JOHN
MACARTHUR

PHILIPPIANS

Christ, the Source of Joy and Strength

THOMAS NELSON
Since 1798

NASHVILLE   DALLAS   MEXICO CITY   RIO DE JANEIRO   BEIJING

Philippians
MacArthur Bible Studies

Copyright © 2007, John MacArthur.

Published by Nelson Impact, a Division of Thomas Nelson, Inc., P.O. Box 141000, Nashville, Tennessee 37214.

Produced with the assistance of the Livingstone Corporation. Project staff include Jake Barton, Mary Horner Collins, and Andy Culbertson.

Project editor: Len Woods

Scripture quotations marked NKJV are taken from *The Holy Bible*, New King James Version˙. Copyright © 1979, 1980, 1982, 1992 Thomas Nelson, Inc. Publishers.

"Keys to the Text" and "Truth for Today" material is taken from the following sources:

Anxiety Attacked. Copyright © 1993 by John MacArthur, Jr. Published by Victor Books, Wheaton, Illinois.

The MacArthur Study Bible (electronic ed.). John MacArthur, General Editor. Copyright © 1997 by Word Publishing. All rights reserved. Used by permission.

Our Sufficiency in Christ. Copyright © 1991 by John MacArthur. Word Publishing, a Division of Thomas Nelson, Inc. Dallas, TX.

Philippians. MacArthur New Testament Commentary Series. Copyright © 2001 by John MacArthur. Published by Moody Press, Chicago, Illinois. Used by permission.

Cover Art by Kirk Luttrell, Livingstone Corporation

Interior Design and Composition by Joel Bartlett, Livingstone Corporation

ISBN-10: 1-4185-0960-4
ISBN-13: 978-1-4185-0960-6

Printed in the United States of America.
08 09 RRD 9 8 7 6 5

CONTENTS

Introduction to Philippians

Philippians derives its name from the Greek city where the church to which it was addressed was located. Philippi was the first town in Macedonia where Paul established a church.

Author and Date

The unanimous testimony of the early church was that the apostle Paul wrote Philippians. Nothing in the letter would have motivated a forger to write it.

The question of when Philippians was written cannot be separated from that of where it was written. The traditional view is that Philippians, along with the other Prison Epistles (Ephesians, Colossians, Philemon), was written during Paul's first imprisonment at Rome (ca. AD 60–62). The most natural understanding of the references to the "palace guard" (1:13) and the "saints . . . of Caesar's household" (4:22) is that Paul wrote from Rome, where the emperor lived. The similarities between the details of Paul's imprisonment given in Acts and in the Prison Epistles also argue that those epistles were written from Rome (e.g., Paul was guarded by soldiers, Acts 28:16; see 1:13–14; was permitted to receive visitors, Acts 28:30; see 4:18; and had the opportunity to preach the gospel, Acts 28:31; see 1:12–14; Eph. 6:18–20; Col. 4:2–4).

Some have held that Paul wrote the Prison Epistles during his two-year imprisonment at Caesarea (Acts 24:27). But Paul's opportunities to receive visitors and proclaim the gospel were severely limited during that imprisonment (see Acts 23:35). The Prison Epistles express Paul's hope for a favorable verdict (1:25; 2:24; see Philem. 22). In Caesarea, however, Paul's only hope for release was either to bribe Felix (Acts 24:26), or agree to stand trial at Jerusalem under Festus (Acts 25:9). In the Prison Epistles, Paul expected the decision in his case to be final (1:20–23; 2:17, 23). That could not have been true at Caesarea, since Paul could and did appeal his case to the emperor.

Another alternative has been that Paul wrote the Prison Epistles from Ephesus. But at Ephesus, like Caesarea, no final decision could be made in his case because of his right to appeal to the emperor. Also, Luke was with Paul when he wrote Colossians (Col. 4:14), but he apparently was not with the apostle at Ephesus. Acts 19, which records Paul's stay in Ephesus, is not in one of the "we" sections of Acts. The most telling argument against Ephesus as the point of origin for the Prison Epistles, however, is that there is no evidence that Paul was ever imprisoned at Ephesus.

In light of the serious difficulties faced by both the Caesarean and Ephesian views, there is no reason to reject the traditional view that Paul wrote the Prison Epistles—including Philippians—from Rome.

Paul's belief that his case would soon be decided (2:23–24) points to Philippians being written toward the close of the apostle's two-year Roman imprisonment (ca. AD 61).

BACKGROUND AND SETTING

Originally known as Krenides ("The Little Fountains") because of the numerous nearby springs, Philippi ("city of Philip") received its name from Philip II of Macedon (the father of Alexander the Great). Attracted by the nearby gold mines, Philip conquered the region in the fourth century BC. In the second century BC, Philippi became part of the Roman province of Macedonia.

The city existed in relative obscurity for the next two centuries until one of the most famous events in Roman history brought it recognition and expansion. In 42 BC, the forces of Antony and Octavian defeated those of Brutus and Cassius at the Battle of Philippi, thus ending the Roman Republic and ushering in the Empire. After the battle, Philippi became a Roman colony (see Acts 16:12), and many veterans of the Roman army settled there. As a colony, Philippi had autonomy from the provincial government and the same rights granted to cities in Italy, including the use of Roman law, exemption from some taxes, and Roman citizenship for its residents (Acts 16:21). Being a colony was also the source of much civic pride for the Philippians, who used Latin as their official language, adopted Roman customs, and modeled their city government after that of Italian cities. Acts and Philippians both reflect Philippi's status as a Roman colony.

Paul's description of Christians as citizens of heaven (3:20) was appropriate, since the Philippians prided themselves on being citizens of Rome (see Acts 16:21). The Philippians may well have known some of the members of the palace guard (1:13) and Caesar's household (4:22).

The church at Philippi, the first one founded by Paul in Europe, dates from the apostle's second missionary journey (Acts 16:12–40). Philippi evidently had a very small Jewish population. Because there were not enough men to form a synagogue (the requirement was for ten Jewish men who were heads of a household), some devout women met outside the city at a place of prayer (Acts 16:13) alongside the Gangites River. Paul preached the gospel to them, and Lydia, a wealthy merchant dealing in expensive purple dyed goods (Acts 16:14), became a believer (16:14–15). It is likely that the Philippian church initially met in her spacious home.

Satanic opposition to the new church immediately arose in the person of a demon-possessed, fortune-telling slave girl (Acts 16:16–17). Not wanting even agreeable testimony from such an evil source, Paul cast the demon out of her (Acts 16:18). The apostle's act enraged the girl's masters, who could no longer sell her services as a fortune-teller (Acts 16:19). They hauled Paul and Silas before the city's magistrates (Acts 16:20) and inflamed the civic pride of the Philippians by claiming the two preachers were a threat to Roman customs (Acts 16:20–21). As a result, Paul and Silas were beaten and imprisoned (Acts 16:22–24).

The two preachers were miraculously released from prison that night by an earthquake, which unnerved the jailer and opened his heart and that of his household to the gospel (Acts 16:25–34). The next day the magistrates, panicking when they learned they had illegally beaten and imprisoned two Roman citizens, begged Paul and Silas to leave Philippi.

Paul apparently visited Philippi twice during his third missionary journey, once at the beginning (see 2 Cor. 8:1–5) and again near the end (Acts 20:6). About four or five years after his last visit to Philippi, while a prisoner at Rome, Paul received a delegation from the Philippian church. The Philippians had generously supported Paul in the past (4:15–16), and had also contributed abundantly for the needy at Jerusalem (2 Cor. 8:1–4). Now, hearing of Paul's imprisonment, they sent another contribution to him (4:10), and along with it, then sent Epaphroditus to minister to Paul's needs. Unfortunately Epaphroditus suffered a near-fatal illness (2:26–27) either while en route to Rome or after he arrived. Accordingly, Paul decided to send Epaphroditus back to Philippi (2:25–26) and wrote the letter to the Philippians to send back with him.

Paul had several purposes in composing this epistle. First, he wanted to express in writing his thanks for the Philippians' gift (4:10–18). Second, he wanted the Philippians to know why he decided to return Epaphroditus to them, so they would not think his service to Paul had been unsatisfactory (2:25–26). Third, he wanted to inform them about his circumstances at Rome (1:12–26). Fourth, he wrote to exhort them to unity (2:1–2; 4:2). Finally, he wrote to warn them against false teachers (3:1–4:1).

HISTORICAL AND THEOLOGICAL THEMES

Since it is primarily a practical letter, Philippians contains little historical material (there are no Old Testament quotes), apart from the momentous treatment of Paul's spiritual autobiography (3:4–7). There is, likewise, little direct theological instruction, also with one momentous exception. The magnificent passage describing Christ's humiliation and exaltation (2:5–11) contains some of the most profound and crucial teaching on the Lord Jesus Christ in all the Bible. The major theme of pursuing Christlikeness, as the most defining element of spiritual growth and the one passion of Paul in his own life, is presented in 3:12–14. In spite of Paul's imprisonment, the dominant tone of the letter is joyful.

INTERPRETIVE CHALLENGES

The major difficulty connected with Philippians is determining where it was written. The text itself presents only one significant interpretive challenge: the identity of the "enemies of the cross." (See the study notes in lesson 10.)

THE EPISTLE OF JOY

DRAWING NEAR

Who is one of the most joyful Christians you know? What do you like about that person?

_____

_____

_____

_____

What situations tend to make you joyful? What situations steal your joy?

_____

_____

_____

_____

THE CONTEXT

If people were to search for joy, they probably would not think to look in prison. But that is where Paul wrote this marvelous letter about joy. Through Paul, the Holy Spirit taught that circumstances don't dictate the quality of joy believers have in Christ. How did Paul find joy in prison? He didn't. He took his joy _in Christ_ into jail with him; therefore, joy was his continual companion.

The love bond between Paul and the Philippian believers may have been stronger than the one he had with any other church. The depth of their relationship encouraged Paul during his imprisonment and added to his joy. He was concerned about their unity, their faithfulness, and many other important spiritual and practical matters. But his overriding desire was that their sorrow over his afflictions would be tempered by their joy over his faithfulness to the Lord. Paul wanted them not to be sad, but to share in the fullest measure his deep, abiding joy in Jesus Christ. It is a noteworthy testimony to the maturity of the Philippian believers that, although Paul warned and encouraged them, he made no mention of any theological or moral problem in the church at Philippi. That also brought the apostle joy.

Keys to the Text

Joy: Paul uses the word *joy* (Greek *chara*) four times in this letter (1:4, 25; 2:2; 4:1). The related verb *rejoice* (Greek *chairo*) appears in the text nine times (1:18, 26; 2:17–18; 3:1; 4:4, 10). In the early chapters, these terms are used primarily to describe Paul's own experience with life in Christ. The beginning of chapter 3, however, is a transition point, shifting to a section of spiritual direction. Paul's expression "rejoice in the Lord" (3:1) is the first time he used the phrase "in the Lord." Unrelated to the circumstances of life, the believers' joy flows from an unassailable, unchanging relationship with the sovereign Lord.

Unleashing the Text

Read 1:1–11, noting the key words and definitions next to the passage.

Philippians 1:1–11 (NKJV)

1 *Paul and Timothy, bondservants of Jesus Christ, to all the saints in Christ Jesus who are in Philippi, with the bishops and deacons:*

2 *Grace to you and peace from God our Father and the Lord Jesus Christ.*

3 *I thank my God upon every remembrance of you,*

4 *always in every prayer of mine making request for you all with joy,*

5 *for your fellowship in the gospel from the first day until now,*

6 *being confident of this very thing, that He who has begun a good work in you will complete it until the day of Jesus Christ;*

Paul (v. 1)—Paul wrote this letter from a Roman prison.

Timothy (v. 1)—Paul's beloved son in the faith; not the co-author of the letter, but possibly the one to whom Paul dictated it.

bondservants (v. 1)—This denotes a willing slave who was happily and loyally linked to his master.

in Christ Jesus (v. 1)—This describes the Philippian believers' union with Christ in His death and resurrection.

bishops (v. 1)—literally, "overseers"; a term used to emphasize the leadership responsibilities of those who are elders, who are also called pastors

deacons (v. 1)—literally, "those who serve"

in every prayer . . . with joy (v. 4)—The Greek word for "prayer" denotes a petition for, or a request made on behalf of, someone else. It was a delight for him to intercede for fellow believers.

fellowship (v. 5)—can also be translated "participation" or "partnership"

from the first day (v. 5)—These believers eagerly assisted Paul in evangelizing Philippi from the beginning of the church there (Acts 16:12–40).

He . . . will complete it (v. 6)—When God begins a work of salvation in a person, He finishes and perfects that work. Thus the verb "will complete" points to the eternal security of the Christian.

day of Jesus Christ (v. 6)—Not to be confused with the "Day of the Lord," which describes final divine judgment and wrath (see Isa. 13:9; Joel 1:15; 2:11; 1 Thess. 5:2; 2 Pet. 3:10). "Day of Jesus Christ" looks to the final salvation, reward, and glorification of believers (see 1 Cor. 3:10–15; 4:5; 2 Cor. 5:9–10).

7   *just as it is right for me to think this of you all,*
    because I have you in my heart, inasmuch as both
    in my chains and in the defense and confirmation
    of the gospel, you all are partakers with me of grace.
8   *For God is my witness, how greatly I long for you all*
    with the affection of Jesus Christ.
9   *And this I pray, that your love may abound still*
    more and more in knowledge and all discernment,
10 *that you may approve the things that are excellent,*
    that you may be sincere and without offense till the
    day of Christ,
11 *being filled with the fruits of righteousness which are*
    by Jesus Christ, to the glory and praise of God.

heart (v. 7)—a common biblical word used to describe the center of thought and feeling (see Prov. 4:23)

partakers with me of grace (v. 7)—During his imprisonment, the Philippians sent money to Paul and offered Epaphroditus's services to support the apostle, thus sharing in God's gracious blessing on his ministry.

affection (v. 8)—The word literally refers to the internal organs, which are the part of the body that reacts to intense emotion. It became the strongest Greek word to express compassionate love—a love that involves one's entire being.

in knowledge (v. 9)—This is from the Greek word that describes genuine, full, or advanced knowledge. Biblical love is not an empty sentimentalism but is anchored and regulated by the truth of Scripture (see Eph. 5:2–3; 1 Peter 1:22).

discernment (v. 9)—Moral perception, insight, and the practical application of knowledge. Love is not blind but perceptive, and it carefully scrutinizes to distinguish between right and wrong.

sincere and without offense (v. 10)—"Sincere" means "genuine," and may have originally meant "tested by sunlight." In the ancient world, dishonest pottery dealers filled cracks in their inferior products with wax before glazing and painting them, making worthless pots difficult to distinguish from expensive ones. The only way to avoid being defrauded was to hold the pot to the sun, making the wax-filled cracks obvious. Dealers marked their fine pottery that could withstand "sun testing" as *sine cera*, "without wax." "Without offense" can be translated "blameless," referring to relational integrity. Christians are to live lives of true integrity that do not cause others to sin.

to the glory and praise of God (v. 11)—The ultimate end of all Paul's prayers was that God be glorified.

1) How did Paul describe himself and Timothy? The Philippian believers?

_____

_____

_____

_____

_____

_____

_____

_____

2) Why was Paul joyful when praying for the Christians in Philippi?

_____

_____

_____

_____

_____

3) What does verse 6 reveal about God's work in our lives?

_____

_____

_____

_____

_____

4) What phrases or words reveal the kind of deep relationship that existed between Paul and this church he had planted only a short time before?

_____

_____

_____

5) Summarize in your own words the content of Paul's prayer for the church at Philippi.

_____

_____

_____

_____

_____

Going Deeper

In all of Paul's recorded prayers, the spiritual issues were of supreme importance. Read Ephesians 1:15–23 for another example of this.

15 *Therefore I also, after I heard of your faith in the Lord Jesus and your love for all the saints,*

16 *do not cease to give thanks for you, making mention of you in my prayers:*

17 *that the God of our Lord Jesus Christ, the Father of glory, may give to you the spirit of wisdom and revelation in the knowledge of Him,*

18 *the eyes of your understanding being enlightened; that you may know what is the hope of His calling, what are the riches of the glory of His inheritance in the saints,*

19 *and what is the exceeding greatness of His power toward us who believe, according to the working of His mighty power*

20 *which He worked in Christ when He raised Him from the dead and seated Him at His right hand in the heavenly places,*

21 *far above all principality and power and might and dominion, and every name that is named, not only in this age but also in that which is to come.*

22 *And He put all things under His feet, and gave Him to be head over all things to the church,*

23 *which is His body, the fullness of Him who fills all in all.*

Exploring the Meaning

6) Why do you think Paul's prayers focused more on the spiritual welfare of others, rather than their physical welfare?

_____

_____

_____

_____

7) What did Paul mean when he spoke of the Philippians' "fellowship" and being partners in the gospel (Phil. 1:5)?

_____

_____

_____

8) How would you distinguish between knowledge, insight, and discernment (vv. 9–10)?

_____

_____

_____

_____

_____

_____

9) Why is it significant that Paul linked love and knowledge? What are the dangers if a person has only one of those traits?

_____

_____

_____

_____

_____

_____

Truth for Today

Most people define happiness as an attitude of satisfaction or delight based on positive circumstances largely beyond their control. Happiness, therefore, cannot be planned or programmed, much less guaranteed. It is experienced only if and when circumstances are favorable. It is therefore elusive and uncertain. Spiritual joy, on the other hand, is not an attitude dependent on chance or circumstances. It is the deep and abiding confidence that, regardless of one's circumstances in life, all is well between the believer and the Lord. No matter what difficulty, pain, disappointment, failure, rejection, or other challenge one is facing, genuine joy remains because of that eternal well-being established by God's grace in salvation. Thus, Scripture makes it clear that the fullest, most lasting and satisfying joy is derived from a true relationship with God. It is not based on circumstances or chance, but is the gracious and permanent possession of every child of God. Therefore it is not surprising that joy is an important New Testament theme.

Reflecting on the Text

10) How can you encourage the overseers (or elders) and deacons at your church this week, causing them to be filled with joy and thanksgiving?

_____

_____

_____

_____

_____

_____

11) As Paul prayed for the Philippians, no doubt, there are people praying for you (a pastor, a small group leader, Sunday school teacher). What can *you* do to see love abound more and more in your life (v. 9)?

_____

_____

_____

_____

_____

_____

_____

_____

12) Surely this letter brought a smile to the faces of the Philippian believers. To whom can you write a letter, card, or e-mail to encourage or express gratitude?

_____

_____

_____

Personal Response

Write out additional reflections, questions you may have, or a prayer.

2

THE JOY OF MINISTRY

Philippians 1:12–26

DRAWING NEAR

Paul found joy in ministry, even when it was difficult. Yet he longed for heaven, knowing that to die is gain. Do you consider it gain to die? Why or why not? What kinds of situations cause you to feel ready to depart this life?

_____

_____

_____

_____

_____

_____

THE CONTEXT

One of the surest measures of our spiritual maturity is what it takes to rob us of our Spirit-bestowed joy. Paul's maturity is evident as he makes it clear that difficult, painful, even life-threatening circumstances did not rob him of joy but rather caused it to increase. Paul certainly experienced sorrow and tears. He suffered grief and disappointment, and he was troubled by sinful, weak, and contentious believers. Yet, there never seems to have been a time in his life as a believer when circumstances diminished his joy. In fact, it seems as if the worst affliction merely tightened his grip on salvation's joy.

Although he was writing this epistle from a private residence, Paul was chained night and day to a Roman soldier while under house arrest. In this section of Philippians, he discusses four issues that might have robbed him of joy: trouble (Paul's imprisonment), detractors (those preachers who sought to elevate themselves at Paul's expense), threat of impending death, and the sorrows of living on in the flesh. In the last analysis, it did not really matter to Paul that he was imprisoned, maligned, and facing possible execution, as long as the saving gospel of Christ was being preached. He was fully confident that, despite his negative circumstances, the Lord's cause would triumph. Therefore, he could face death without fear.

13

Keys to the Text

Supply: This Greek word was used to describe what a choir manager would provide for the members of a Greek choir who performed in Greek drama. In short, he took care of all their living expenses. The word came to mean a full supply of any kind. The Philippians' prayer would generate the Spirit's supply (1:19). Paul was looking forward to getting a full supply of Jesus Christ's Spirit as a result of the Philippians' prayers.

Progress: This word describes not merely moving ahead but doing so against obstacles (1:25). The related verb was used of an explorer or of an army advance team hacking a path through dense trees and underbrush, moving ahead slowly and with considerable effort. Resistance is therefore inherent to that sort of progress, and no one knew better than Paul how inevitable the resistance of Satan and the world is to the progress of the gospel. Far from lamenting, resenting, or complaining about his various hardships, Paul acknowledged them as an unavoidable element of ministry. They were a small cost that he was more than willing to pay as a means for furthering the progress of the gospel.

Unleashing the Text

Read 1:12–26, noting the key words and definitions next to the passage.

Philippians 1:12–26 (NKJV)

things which happened to me (v. 12)—Paul's difficult circumstances, namely, his journey to Rome and imprisonment there

evident . . . chains are in Christ (v. 13)—People around him recognized that Paul was no criminal, but had become a prisoner because of preaching Jesus Christ and the gospel (see Eph. 6:20).

whole palace guard (v. 13)— The Greek word for "palace,"

12 *But I want you to know, brethren, that the things which happened to me have actually turned out for the furtherance of the gospel,*

13 *so that it has become evident to the whole palace guard, and to all the rest, that my chains are in Christ;*

14 *and most of the brethren in the Lord, having become confident by my chains, are much more bold to speak the word without fear.*

often simply used in its transliterated form *praetorion,* can denote either a special building (e.g., a commander's headquarters, the emperor's palace) or the group of men in the Imperial guard. Because Paul was in a private house in Rome, "palace guard" probably refers to the members of the Imperial guard who guarded Paul day and night (see Acts 28:16).

all the rest (v. 13)—everyone else in the city of Rome who met and heard him (see Acts 28:23–24, 30–31)

much more bold to speak (v. 14)—Paul's example of powerful witness to the gospel as a prisoner demonstrated God's faithfulness and encouraged others to be bold and not fear imprisonment.

15 *Some indeed preach Christ even from envy and strife, and some also from goodwill:*

16 *The former preach Christ from selfish ambition, not sincerely, supposing to add affliction to my chains;*

17 *but the latter out of love, knowing that I am appointed for the defense of the gospel.*

18 *What then? Only that in every way, whether in pretense or in truth, Christ is preached; and in this I rejoice, yes, and will rejoice.*

19 *For I know that this will turn out for my deliverance through your prayer and the supply of the Spirit of Jesus Christ,*

20 *according to my earnest expectation and hope that in nothing I shall be ashamed, but with all boldness, as always, so now also Christ will be magnified in my body, whether by life or by death.*

21 *For to me, to live is Christ, and to die is gain.*

22 *But if I live on in the flesh, this will mean fruit from my labor; yet what I shall choose I cannot tell.*

23 *For I am hard-pressed between the two, having a desire to depart and be with Christ, which is far better.*

24 *Nevertheless to remain in the flesh is more needful for you.*

25 *And being confident of this, I know that I shall remain and continue with you all for your progress and joy of faith,*

26 *that your rejoicing for me may be more abundant in Jesus Christ by my coming to you again.*

from envy and strife (v. 15)—This describes the attitude of Paul's detractors, who preached the gospel but were jealous of his apostolic power, authority, success, and immense giftedness. "Strife" connotes contention, rivalry, and conflict, which resulted when Paul's critics began discrediting him.

selfish ambition (v. 16)—This describes those who were interested only in self-advancement, or who ruthlessly sought to get ahead at any cost.

not sincerely (v. 16)—Paul's preacher critics did not have pure motives.

appointed (v. 17)—The Greek word describes a soldier's being placed on duty. Paul was in prison because he was destined to be there by God's will, so as to be in a strategic position to proclaim the gospel.

I rejoice . . . will rejoice (v. 18)—Paul was glad when the gospel was proclaimed with authority, no matter who received credit. He endured the unjust accusations without bitterness at his accusers. Rather, he rejoiced that they preached Christ, even in a pretense of godliness.

my deliverance (v. 19)—"Deliverance" is from the basic Greek term for salvation. But it can also be rendered "well-being" or "escape."

Spirit of Jesus Christ (v. 19)—The Holy Spirit (Rom. 8:9; Gal. 4:6). Paul had supreme confidence in the Spirit.

to me, to live is Christ (v. 21)—For Paul, life is summed up in Jesus Christ; Christ was his reason for being.

to die is gain (v. 21)—Death would relieve him of earthly burdens and let him focus totally on glorifying God.

the flesh (v. 22)—Here this word does not refer to one's fallen humanness (as in Rom. 7:5, 18; 8:1), but simply to physical life (as in 2 Cor. 10:3; Gal. 2:20).

hard-pressed (v. 23)—The Greek word pictures a traveler on a narrow path, a rock wall on either side allowing him to go only straight ahead.

more needful for you (v. 24)—Paul yielded his personal desire to be with his Lord for the necessity of the building of the church (see 2:3–4).

1) How did Paul's incarceration affect the Philippian believers?

_____

_____

_____

_____

2) How did his imprisonment affect other preachers who jealously viewed Paul as a rival?

_____

_____

_____

3) List the various words and phrases that reveal Paul's motives and attitudes.

_____

_____

_____

_____

4) Put verse 21 in your own words. What is the idea Paul is conveying here?

_____

_____

_____

_____

_____

_____

_____

5) In what specific ways was Paul torn emotionally and spiritually?

_____

_____

_____

_____

_____

Going Deeper

Though Paul was well acquainted with suffering, nothing seemed to dim his love for God or his commitment to take the gospel to the ends of the earth. Read Colossians 1:24–29.

24 *I now rejoice in my sufferings for you, and fill up in my flesh what is lacking in the afflictions of Christ, for the sake of His body, which is the church,*

25 *of which I became a minister according to the stewardship from God which was given to me for you, to fulfill the word of God,*

26 *the mystery which has been hidden from ages and from generations, but now has been revealed to His saints.*

27 *To them God willed to make known what are the riches of the glory of this mystery among the Gentiles: which is Christ in you, the hope of glory.*

28 *Him we preach, warning every man and teaching every man in all wisdom, that we may present every man perfect in Christ Jesus.*

29 *To this end I also labor, striving according to His working which works in me mightily.*

Exploring the Meaning

6) How do Paul's words to the Colossians echo his honest comments in Philippians 1:12–26?

_____

_____

_____

_____

17

7) Bible scholars recognize four possible interpretations of Paul's confident hope of salvation or deliverance (Phil 1:19). It could refer to Paul's ultimate salvation, to his temporal deliverance from execution, to being vindicated by the emperor's ruling, or to his eventual release from prison. Which of these interpretations do you find most plausible, and why?

_____

_____

_____

_____

_____

_____

_____

8) How specifically does one develop the maturity and faith to be able to face painful circumstances with a positive, hopeful attitude?

_____

_____

_____

_____

_____

9) What does it mean to be able to say, with all genuineness, "For to me, to live is Christ"?

_____

_____

_____

_____

_____

_____

Truth for Today

Although joy is a gift from God to every believer and administered by the Holy Spirit (Gal. 5:22), joy is not always constant and full. The only certain cause for loss of joy in a believer's life is sin, which corrupts his fellowship with the Lord, who is the source of joy. Such sinful attitudes as dissatisfaction, bitterness, sullenness, doubt, fear, and negativism cause joy to be forfeited.

Anything other than sin—no matter how difficult, painful, or disappointing—need not take away the believer's joy. Yet even minor things can do so if believers react sinfully to them. A change for the worse in health, job, finances, personal relationships, or other important areas of life can easily cause believers to question God's sovereign wisdom and gracious provision. When that happens, joy is one of the first casualties. Believers are especially vulnerable when such things happen suddenly, taking them off guard. In such cases, events lead to sinful responses that steal joy. Consequently, the only way to restore lost joy is to repent and return to proper worship of and obedience to God.

Reflecting on the Text

10) Think of potentially disappointing situations in your life, or certain trials that may loom ahead. List some possible wrong reactions to each difficulty. Finally, list some specific joy-filled, God-honoring responses.

Situation	Immature Reaction	Mature Response

11) Paul mentioned his desire to engage in fruitful labor. What would this look like in your life?

_____

_____

_____

_____

_____

12) Think of someone in your sphere of influence who is going through a hard time and maybe has lost his or her joy. How can you encourage that person this week?

_____

_____

_____

_____

Personal Response

Write out additional reflections, questions you may have, or a prayer.

_____

_____

_____

_____

_____

_____

_____

_____

_____

_____

CONDUCT WORTHY OF CHRIST

3

Philippians 1:27–30

DRAWING NEAR

To begin thinking about this lesson's topic, put a check by the twelve qualities or practices that you consider the *most indispensable* in living a life worthy of Christ. (Remember, you may only check twelve things.)

___ joy	___ theological knowledge	___ compassion
___ discernment	___ witnessing ability	___ zeal
___ love for Christ	___ love for fellow Christians	___ love for the lost
___ wisdom	___ involvement in local church	___ devotion to prayer
___ strong faith	___ a global missions mind-set	___ endurance
___ peace	___ a desire to be a peacemaker	___ patience
___ hospitality	___ a willingness to suffer	___ faithfulness
___ a servant mind-set	___ generosity in giving	___ self-control
___ a grateful heart	___ a hunger for the truth	___ Other:

THE CONTEXT

Paul had a special love, respect, and appreciation for the church at Philippi. It was one of the most mature of the churches described in the New Testament. Nevertheless, its members had a few problems, some of them potentially serious. Like every church in every age, they needed to be on guard against false teachers and repudiate those in the congregation who were "enemies of the cross of Christ" (3:18 NKJV). The apostle knew that it does not take long even for a faithful church to slip into indifference and eventually into moral and doctrinal error.

Paul turned from the autobiographical emphasis in the first part of the letter to focus on the Philippian congregation. He called on them to maintain their spiritual commitment and conduct themselves in a way that is consistent with the power of the gospel. He told them to look carefully into their own hearts to determine if they have spiritual integrity. This appeal applies to every follower of Jesus Christ in every place and time.

Keys to the Text

Conduct: Philippians 1:27–30 is one long sentence in the Greek, and *politeuomai* ("conduct") is the main verb. It comes from the root word *polis* ("city"), which in earlier times usually referred to the city-states. The verb carries the basic meaning of being a citizen. But, by implication, it means being a *good* citizen, one whose conduct brings honor to the political body to whom one belongs. Philippi had the distinction of being a Roman colony, a highly privileged status that gave its inhabitants many of the rights enjoyed by citizens of Rome itself. A responsible citizen was careful not to do anything that would bring disrepute on his *polis.* And he tried always to be considered an honorable citizen, so that he would never be removed from the list of citizens. Paul may have had that sense of dedication in mind in using the term *politeuomai* ("to conduct"). If the citizens of Philippi were so devoted to the honor of their human kingdom, how much more should believers be devoted to the kingdom of Christ?

Unleashing the Text

Read 1:27–30, noting the key words and definitions next to the passage.

Philippians 1:27–30 (NKJV)

worthy of the gospel (v. 27)—Believers are to have integrity, i.e., to live consistently with what they believe, teach, and preach.

one spirit . . . one mind (v. 27)—This introduces Paul's theme of unity that continues through 2:4. His call for genuine unity of heart and mind is based on (1) the necessity of oneness to win the spiritual battle for the faith (vv. 28–30); (2) the love of others in the fellowship (2:1–2); (3) genuine humility and self-sacrifice (2:3–4); and (4) the example of Jesus Christ, who proved that sacrifice produces eternal glory (2:5–11).

27 *Only let your conduct be worthy of the gospel of Christ, so that whether I come and see you or am absent, I may hear of your affairs, that you stand fast in one spirit, with one mind striving together for the faith of the gospel,*

28 *and not in any way terrified by your adversaries, which is to them a proof of perdition, but to you of salvation, and that from God.*

29 *For to you it has been granted on behalf of Christ, not only to believe in Him, but also to suffer for His sake,*

striving together (v. 27)—Literally, "to struggle along with someone." Paul changed the metaphor from that of a soldier standing at his post ("stand fast") to one of a team struggling for victory against a common foe.

the faith of the gospel (v. 27)—the Christian faith as revealed by God and recorded in the Scripture (Jude 3; see Rom. 1:1; Gal. 1:7)

proof of perdition (v. 28)—When believers willingly suffer without being "terrified," it is a sign that God's enemies will be destroyed and eternally lost.

granted . . . to suffer (v. 29)—The Greek verb translated "granted" is from the noun for "grace." Believers' suffering is a gift of grace, which brings power and eternal reward.

30 *having the same conflict which you saw in me and now hear is in me.*

same conflict (v. 30)—the same kind of suffering Paul had experienced (vv. 12–14; Acts 16:22–24)

you saw (v. 30)—This refers to what the Philippians witnessed when Paul and Silas were imprisoned at Philippi (Acts 16:19–40).

1) What was Paul's command to the Philippian believers (v. 27)? What is significant about the verb he chose?

_____

_____

_____

_____

2) What descriptive phrases of "worthy conduct" did Paul use to refer to a unified body of believers?

_____

_____

_____

_____

3) Rather than competing against one another, what did Paul suggest in verse 27?

_____

_____

_____

_____

_____

_____

_____

4) For what two reasons did Paul say it was unnecessary for the Philippians to fear their opponents?

_____

_____

_____

_____

5) What is the sobering promise of verse 29?

_____

_____

_____

_____

Going Deeper

Paul was concerned that Christians not only believe the right things, but that they also behave the right way. Read about the expected behavior of believers in Romans 12:9–21.

9 *Let love be without hypocrisy. Abhor what is evil. Cling to what is good.*
10 *Be kindly affectionate to one another with brotherly love, in honor giving preference to one another;*
11 *not lagging in diligence, fervent in spirit, serving the Lord;*
12 *rejoicing in hope, patient in tribulation, continuing steadfastly in prayer;*
13 *distributing to the needs of the saints, given to hospitality.*
14 *Bless those who persecute you; bless and do not curse.*
15 *Rejoice with those who rejoice, and weep with those who weep.*
16 *Be of the same mind toward one another. Do not set your mind on high things, but associate with the humble. Do not be wise in your own opinion.*
17 *Repay no one evil for evil. Have regard for good things in the sight of all men.*
18 *If it is possible, as much as depends on you, live peaceably with all men.*
19 *Beloved, do not avenge yourselves, but rather give place to wrath; for it is written, "Vengeance is Mine, I will repay," says the Lord.*

20 *Therefore "If your enemy is hungry, feed him; if he is thirsty, give him a drink; for in so doing you will heap coals of fire on his head."*

21 *Do not be overcome by evil, but overcome evil with good.*

EXPLORING THE MEANING

6) In what ways would the conduct prescribed by Paul in Romans 12 be "worthy of the gospel of Christ"?

_____

_____

_____

_____

_____

7) What positive results did Paul expect from the Philippian believers who stood firm and worked together? What is the goal of this way of living?

_____

_____

_____

_____

_____

_____

8) *Striving together* in the church means playing as a team to advance the truth of God. What are some specific ways the church can strive together to advance God's kingdom? What are some of the enemy forces we face?

_____

_____

_____

_____

_____

9) When Paul mentions suffering (v. 29), the idea is that in His sovereign grace, God grants believers the privilege of suffering for His sake. How can suffering be a gracious gift or privilege?

_____

_____

_____

_____

_____

_____

Truth for Today

The Church's greatest testimony before the world is spiritual integrity. When Christians live below the standards of biblical morality and reverence for their Lord, they compromise the full biblical truth concerning the character, plan, and will of God. By so doing, they seriously weaken the credibility of the gospel and lessen their impact on the world. When the unsaved look at the church and do not see holiness, purity, and virtue, there appears to be no reason to believe the gospel it proclaims. When pastors commit gross sins and are later restored to positions of leadership in the church; when church members lie, steal, cheat, gossip, and quarrel; and when congregations seem to care little about such sin and hypocrisy in their midst, the world is understandably repulsed by their claims to love and serve God. And the name of Christ is sullied and dishonored.

Reflecting on the Text

10) Church strife is often generated by holding grudges, unjust criticism, bitterness, dissatisfaction, and distrust. Think about your own church community. How can you work to heal church strife?

_____

_____

_____

_____

11) Consider the situations you will face this week. How can you stand firm in your convictions? What will that look like in your life?

_____

_____

_____

_____

_____

_____

12) What is the one principle you are taking away from this lesson that will help you become a person of spiritual integrity? Why does this particular truth stand out to you?

_____

_____

_____

_____

_____

PERSONAL RESPONSE

Write out additional reflections, questions you may have, or a prayer.

_____

_____

_____

_____

_____

_____

_____

Additional Notes

~ 4 ~
SPIRITUAL UNITY

DRAWING NEAR

We all long for unity. But even the most doctrinally sound and spiritually mature church is not immune to the threat of selfishness, and nothing can more quickly divide and weaken a church. What are some subtle ways selfishness is manifested in the church at large today?

_____

_____

_____

_____

THE CONTEXT

The church at Philippi was theologically sound, devoted, moral, loving, zealous, courageous, prayerful, and generous. Yet it faced the danger of discord that often is generated by only a few people. Such troublemakers can stir up the contention and strife that fractures an entire congregation. And because disunity is so tragically debilitating, Paul gently but firmly pleads with believers to be constantly and diligently on guard against it. He had just expressed to the Philippians his hope to hear that they "stand fast in one spirit, with one mind striving together for the faith of the gospel" (1:27 NKJV).

In this section Paul gives what is perhaps the most concise and practical teaching about unity in the New Testament. In these four powerful verses, he outlines a formula for spiritual unity that includes three necessary elements on which that unity must be built: the right motives, the right marks, and the right means.

KEYS TO THE TEXT

Consolation: This word can also be translated "encouragement," and is from the Greek word _paraklesis_ that means "to come alongside and help, counsel, exhort." Using a closely related word in John 14:16, Jesus referred to the Holy Spirit as "another Helper" (_parakleton_). The most important and powerful encouragement in Christ comes directly from the indwelling Spirit. Paul's admonition here is that, in light of that encouragement, the Philippians endeavor to be of one mind and spirit with one another. This profound spiritual principle demands pursuing unity as a grateful response to the believer's union with Christ. Paul asks, in effect, "Shouldn't the divine influence of Christ in your life compel you to preserve the unity that is so precious to Him?"

UNLEASHING THE TEXT

Read 2:1–4, noting the key words and definitions next to the passage.

comfort of love (v. 1)—The Greek word translated "comfort" portrays the Lord coming close and whispering words of gentle cheer or tender counsel in a believer's ear.

fellowship of the Spirit (v. 1)—"Fellowship" refers to the partnership believers have with each other based on their common hope of eternal life, a partnership that is provided by the indwelling Holy Spirit.

affection and mercy (v. 1)—God has extended His deep affection and compassion to every believer (see Rom. 12:1; 2 Cor. 1:3; Col. 3:12), and that reality should result in unity.

Philippians 2:1–4 (NKJV)

1 *Therefore if there is any consolation in Christ, if any comfort of love, if any fellowship of the Spirit, if any affection and mercy,*

2 *fulfill my joy by being like-minded, having the same love, being of one accord, of one mind.*

3 *Let nothing be done through selfish ambition or conceit, but in lowliness of mind let each esteem others better than himself.*

4 *Let each of you look out not only for his own interests, but also for the interests of others.*

fulfill my joy (v. 2)—This can also be translated "make my joy complete." Paul's joy was tied to concern for the unity of believers.

like-minded (v. 2)—The Greek word means "think the same way." This exhortation is not optional or obscure, but is repeated throughout the New Testament (see Rom. 15:5; 1 Cor. 1:10; 2 Cor. 13:11–13).

same love (v. 2)—Believers are to love others in the body of Christ equally—not because they are all equally attractive, but by showing the same kind of sacrificial, loving service to all, which was shown to them by Christ (John 15:13).

one accord (v. 2)—This may also be translated "united in spirit" and perhaps is a term specially coined by Paul. It literally means "one-souled" and describes people who are knit together in harmony, having the same desires, passions, and ambitions.

one mind (v. 2)—"Intent on one purpose" is an alternative translation.

selfish ambition (v. 3)—This Greek word, which is sometimes rendered "strife" because it refers to factionalism, rivalry, and partisanship, speaks of the pride that prompts people to push for their own way.

conceit (v. 3)—Literally "empty glory," and often translated "empty conceit." This word refers to the pursuit of personal glory, which is the motivation for selfish ambition.

lowliness of mind (v. 3)—This translates a Greek word that Paul and other New Testament writers apparently coined. It was a term of derision, with the idea of being low, shabby, and humble (see 1 Cor. 15:9; 1 Tim. 1:15).

esteem others better than himself (v. 3)—the basic definition of true humility (see Rom. 12:10; Gal. 5:13; Eph. 5:21; 1 Pet. 5:5)

1) What are the four marks of unity that Paul listed?

2) How did Paul say the Philippians could complete his joy?

like minded - think the same way
same love - seeing others as equal recipients of God's mercy
one accord - Knit together having same desires, ambitions &
one mind - intent on one purpose   passion
                                                    desires

3) If you were teaching this passage to others, how would you explain the following phrases?

— Like-minded

— Same love

— One accord

— One mind

4) Delineate the difference between *conceit* and *lowliness of mind*.

Conceit = pursuit of personal glory
lowliness of mind = low, shabby & humble

Conceit would be self promotion as good, or better than others, more spiritual lowliness of mind seeing our righteousness as filthy rags

5) Summarize Paul's comments about self-centeredness (vv. 3–4).

GOING DEEPER

The unity of the people of God was also on Jesus' heart. Read His prayer in John 17:1, 11–26 to get a sense of Christ's desire for His people to be one.

1 *Jesus spoke these words, lifted up His eyes to heaven, and said: "Father, the hour has come. Glorify Your Son, that Your Son also may glorify You, . . .*

11 *Now I am no longer in the world, but these are in the world, and I come to You. Holy Father, keep through Your name those whom You have given Me, that they may be one as We are.*

12 *While I was with them in the world, I kept them in Your name. Those whom You gave Me I have kept; and none of them is lost except the son of perdition, that the Scripture might be fulfilled.*

13 *But now I come to You, and these things I speak in the world, that they may have My joy fulfilled in themselves.*

14 *I have given them Your word; and the world has hated them because they are not of the world, just as I am not of the world.*

15 *I do not pray that You should take them out of the world, but that You should keep them from the evil one.*

16 *They are not of the world, just as I am not of the world.*

17 *Sanctify them by Your truth. Your word is truth.*

18 *As You sent Me into the world, I also have sent them into the world.*

19 *And for their sakes I sanctify Myself, that they also may be sanctified by the truth.*

20 *"I do not pray for these alone, but also for those who will believe in Me through their word;*

21 *that they all may be one, as You, Father, are in Me, and I in You; that they also may be one in Us, that the world may believe that You sent Me.*

22 *And the glory which You gave Me I have given them, that they may be one just as We are one:*

23 *I in them, and You in Me; that they may be made perfect in one, and that the world may know that You have sent Me, and have loved them as You have loved Me.*

24 *"Father, I desire that they also whom You gave Me may be with Me where I am, that they may behold My glory which You have given Me; for You loved Me before the foundation of the world.*

25 *O righteous Father! The world has not known You, but I have known You; and these have known that You sent Me.*

26 *And I have declared to them Your name, and will declare it, that the love with which You loved Me may be in them, and I in them."*

EXPLORING THE MEANING

6) How did Jesus describe His oneness with His Father?

had God's word & relayed it on, focus not on worldly standards, set apart by having God's word knowing He was sent to go into the world & share knowledge & relationship to God

7) What does Jesus' prayer in John 17 add to your understanding of the meaning of true spiritual unity?

33

8) Paul called for the Philippians to be "like-minded." How can believers do this and yet retain their God-given diversity? How does this work when Spirit-filled Christians truly do not see eye-to-eye about an issue?

like minded - think the same way
examples same goals but give others personal
freedom to accomplish different wAys
ie Billy Graham Crusade - John Jacobs Power
Team
puppet show - revival
Summer Festival - ?

TRUTH FOR TODAY

Selfishness is a consuming and destructive sin. Because this sin, like every other, begins in a sinful heart, anyone can commit it—regardless of whether there is an opportunity for it to be outwardly expressed. Even when not outwardly manifested, selfishness breeds anger, resentment, and jealousy. Selfish ambition is often clothed in pious rhetoric by those who are convinced of their own superior abilities in promoting the cause of Christ. Discord and division are inevitable when people focus on their agendas to the exclusion of others in the church. Often such a narrow focus arises out of genuine passion for an important ministry. But disregard of fellow believers, no matter how unintentional, is a mark of loveless, sinful indifference that produces jealousy, contention, strife, and the other enemies of spiritual unity. Endeavoring to maintain the spiritual unity of a congregation is easily the most pressing, difficult, and constant challenge for its leaders.

REFLECTING ON THE TEXT

9) Do you tend to focus on areas of agreement with other believers, or do you immediately notice and dwell on differences? Why?

Some has to do with personality & gifts
perciever/exhorter (me) helper, teacher,
administrator
ie - teacher - can use almost anything as an
object less
administrator - come up with a sop
helper -

10) Paul warned against "conceit." How can you show humility in your relationships this week? Be specific.

Conceit = empty glory = pursuit of personal glory
~~glory~~

11) What practical steps can you take today to be more selfless and less selfish?

Personal Response

Write out additional reflections, questions you may have, or a prayer.

Additional Notes

~ 5 ~
THE INCARNATION AND
EXALTATION OF CHRIST

Philippians 2:5–11

DRAWING NEAR

There have been numerous cinematic versions of the life of Christ. Which of these (if any) have had a powerful impact on your life? Why?

_____

_____

_____

_____

What aspects of the story of Christ's birth do you find most fascinating, and why?

_____

_____

_____

_____

_____

THE CONTEXT

The Incarnation is the central miracle of Christianity, the most grand and wonderful of all the things that God has ever done. That miracle of miracles is the theme of Philippians 2:5–11. Some scholars believe this passage was originally a hymn sung by early Christians to commemorate and celebrate the incarnation of the Son of God. It has been called a Christological gem, a theological diamond that perhaps sparkles brighter than any other in Scripture. In a simple, brief, yet extraordinarily profound way, it describes the condescension of the second Person of the Trinity to be born, to live, and to die in human form to provide redemption for fallen mankind.

37

Yet as theologically profound and unfathomable as this passage is, it is also an ethical passage. Paul was not merely describing the Incarnation to reveal its theological truths, magnificent as those are. He presents the supreme, unparalleled example of humility to serve as the most powerful motive to believers' humility. The Incarnation calls believers to follow Jesus' incomparable example of humble self-denial, self-giving, self-sacrifice, and selfless love as He lived out the Incarnation in obedient submission to His Father's will.

KEYS TO THE TEXT

Incarnation: A theological term for the coming of God's Son into the world as a human being. The term itself is not used in the Bible, but it is based on clear references in the New Testament to Jesus taking the "form of God" (Phil. 2:6 NKJV). The word *form* comes from the Greek word *morphe*, which was generally used to express the way a thing exists according to what it is *in itself.* Thus, the expression "form of God" may be correctly understood as the essential nature and character of God. To say, therefore, that Christ existed in "the form of God" is to say that apart from His human nature, Christ possessed all the characteristics and qualities belonging to God because He is, in fact, God.

UNLEASHING THE TEXT

Read 2:5–11, noting the key words and definitions next to the passage.

Philippians 2:5–11 (NKJV)

5 *Let this mind be in you which was also in Christ Jesus,*

6 *who, being in the form of God, did not consider it robbery to be equal with God,*

being in the form of God (v. 6)—Paul affirms that Jesus eternally has been God. The usual Greek word for "being" is not used here. Instead, Paul chose another term that stresses the essence of a person's nature—his continuous state or condition. Paul also could have chosen one of two Greek words for "form," but he chose the one that specifically denotes the essential, unchanging character of something—what it is in and of itself. The fundamental doctrine of Christ's deity has always encompassed these crucial characteristics (see John 1:1, 3–4, 14; 8:58; Col. 1:15–17; Heb. 1:3).

not . . . robbery (v. 6)—The Greek word is translated "robbery" here because it originally meant "a thing seized by robbery." It eventually came to mean anything clutched, embraced, or prized, and thus is sometimes translated "grasped" or "held on to." Though Christ had all the rights, privileges, and honors of deity—which He was worthy of and could never be disqualified from—His attitude was not to cling to those things or His position but to be willing to give them up for a season.

equal with God (v. 6)—The Greek word for "equal" defines things that are exactly the same in size, quantity, quality, character, and number. In every sense, Jesus is equal to God and constantly claimed to be so during His earthly ministry (see John 5:18; 10:33, 38; 14:9; 20:28; Heb. 1:1–3).

7 *but made Himself of no reputation, taking the form of a bondservant, and coming in the likeness of men.*

8 *And being found in appearance as a man, He humbled Himself and became obedient to the point of death, even the death of the cross.*

9 *Therefore God also has highly exalted Him and given Him the name which is above every name,*

made Himself of no reputation (v. 7)—This is more clearly translated "emptied Himself." From this Greek word comes the theological word *kenosis*; i.e., the doctrine of Christ's self-emptying in His incarnation. This was a self-renunciation, not an emptying Himself of deity nor an exchange of deity for humanity. Jesus did, however, renounce or set aside His privileges in several areas: (1) heavenly glory—while on earth He gave up the glory of a face-to-face relationship with God and the continuous outward display and personal enjoyment of that glory (see John 17:5); (2) independent authority—during His incarnation Christ completely submitted Himself to the will of His Father (see Matt. 26:39; John 5:30; Heb. 5:8); (3) divine prerogatives—He set aside the voluntary display of His divine attributes and submitted Himself to the Spirit's direction (see Matt. 24:36; John 1:45–49); (4) eternal riches—while on earth Christ was poor and owned very little (see 2 Cor. 8:9); and (5) a favorable relationship with God—He felt the Father's wrath for human sin while on the cross (see Matt. 27:46).

form of a bondservant (v. 7)—Again, Paul uses the Greek word *form*, which indicates exact essence. As a true servant, Jesus submissively did the will of His Father (see Isa. 52:13–14).

the likeness of men (v. 7)—Christ became more than God in a human body, but He took on all the essential attributes of humanity (Luke 2:52; Gal. 4:4; Col. 1:22), even to the extent that He identified with basic human needs and weaknesses (see Heb. 2:14, 17; 4:15). He became the God-Man: fully God and fully man.

in appearance as a man (v. 8)—This is not simply a repetition of the last phrase in v. 7, but a shift from the heavenly focus to an earthly one. Christ's humanity is described from the viewpoint of those who saw Him. Paul is implying that although He outwardly looked like a man, there was much more to Him (His deity) than many people recognized naturally (see John 6:42; 8:48).

He humbled Himself (v. 8)—After the humbling of incarnation, Jesus further humbled Himself in that He did not demand normal human rights, but subjected Himself to persecution and suffering at the hands of unbelievers (see Isa. 53:7; Matt. 26:62–64; Mark 14:60–61; 1 Pet. 2:23).

obedient . . . death (v. 8)—Beyond even persecution, Jesus sank to the lowest point in His humiliation by dying as a criminal, which was according to God's plan for Him (see Matt. 26:39; Acts 2:23).

the cross (v. 8)— Jesus' humiliation was intensified because His death was not by ordinary means, but was accomplished by crucifixion—the cruelest, most excruciating, most degrading form of death ever devised. The Jews hated this manner of execution (Deut. 21:23).

Therefore God (v. 9)—Christ's humiliation (vv. 5–8) and exaltation by God (vv. 9–11) are causally and inseparably linked.

highly exalted Him (v. 9)—Christ's exaltation was fourfold. The early sermons of the apostles affirm His resurrection and coronation (His position at the right hand of God), and allude to His intercession for believers (Acts 2:32–33; 5:30–31; see Eph. 1:20–21; Heb. 4:15; 7:25–26). Hebrews 4:14 refers to the final element, His ascension. The exaltation did not concern Christ's nature or eternal place within the Trinity, but His new identity as the God-Man (see John 5:22; Rom. 1:4; 14:9; 1 Cor. 15:24–25). In addition to receiving back His glory (John 17:5), Christ's new status as the God-Man meant God gave Him privileges He did not have prior to the Incarnation. If He had not lived among men, He could not have identified with them as the interceding High Priest. Had He not died on the cross, He could not have been elevated from that lowest degree back to heaven as the substitute for sin.

name . . . above every name (v. 9)—Christ's new name is "Lord," which further describes His essential nature and places Him above and beyond all comparison. This name is the New Testament synonym for Old Testament descriptions of God as sovereign Ruler. Scripture affirms that this was Jesus' rightful title as the God-Man.

bow . . . confess (vv. 10–11)— The entire intelligent universe is called to worship Jesus Christ as Lord (see Ps. 2). This mandate includes the angels in heaven (Rev. 4:2–9), the spirits of the redeemed (Rev. 4:10–11), obedient believers on earth (Rom. 10:9), the disobedient rebels on earth (2 Thess. 1:7–9), demons and lost humanity in hell (1 Pet. 3:18–22). The Greek word for "confess" means "to acknowledge," "affirm," or "agree," which is what everyone will eventually do in response to Christ's lordship, willingly and blessedly or unwillingly and painfully.

at the name of Jesus (v. 10)— "Jesus" was the name bestowed at His birth (Matt. 1:21), not His new name. The name for Jesus given in the fullest sense after His exaltation was "Lord."

Lord (v. 11)—"Lord" primarily refers to the right to rule, and in the New Testament it denotes mastery over or ownership of people and property. When applied to Jesus, it certainly implies His deity, but it mainly refers to sovereign authority.

glory of God the Father (v. 11)—the purpose of Christ's exaltation (see Matt. 17:5; John 5:23; 13:31–32; 1 Cor. 15:28)

10 *that at the name of Jesus every knee should bow, of those in heaven, and of those on earth, and of those under the earth,*

11 *and that every tongue should confess that Jesus Christ is Lord, to the glory of God the Father.*

1) More than just a hymn of praise, this passage calls believers to *do* something. What?

Let this mind be in you

2) What phrases did Paul use to point to the deity of Christ?

form of God
equal of God
every knee bow
every tongue confess
is Lord

3) What phrases in this passage confirm the true humanity of Jesus?

no reputation

bond servant - slave willing to stay

likeness of men

appearance as a man

obedient to point of death

4) In what specific ways did Christ humble Himself?

layed aside glory

bond servant

appearance of man. nothing more

obedient to death - giving up his life

5) How did Paul describe God the Father's exaltation of Christ?

name above every name

every knee shall bow

every tongue confess

Going Deeper

Only a few people adored Jesus Christ when He first appeared in the world (see Luke 2). Read Revelation 5:6–14 for another perspective on Christ's future lordship and glory.

6   *And I looked, and behold, in the midst of the throne and of the four living creatures, and in the midst of the elders, stood a Lamb as though it had been slain, having seven horns and seven eyes, which are the seven Spirits of God sent out into all the earth.*

7   *Then He came and took the scroll out of the right hand of Him who sat on the throne.*

8   *Now when He had taken the scroll, the four living creatures and the twenty-four elders fell down before the Lamb, each having a harp, and golden bowls full of incense, which are the prayers of the saints.*

9   *And they sang a new song, saying: "You are worthy to take the scroll, and to open its seals; for You were slain, and have redeemed us to God by Your blood out of every tribe and tongue and people and nation,*

10   *And have made us kings and priests to our God; and we shall reign on the earth."*

11   *Then I looked, and I heard the voice of many angels around the throne, the living creatures, and the elders; and the number of them was ten thousand times ten thousand, and thousands of thousands,*

12   *saying with a loud voice: "Worthy is the Lamb who was slain to receive power and riches and wisdom, and strength and honor and glory and blessing!"*

13   *And every creature which is in heaven and on the earth and under the earth and such as are in the sea, and all that are in them, I heard saying: "Blessing and honor and glory and power be to Him who sits on the throne, and to the Lamb, forever and ever!"*

14   *Then the four living creatures said, "Amen!" And the twenty-four elders fell down and worshiped Him who lives forever and ever.*

Exploring the Meaning

6) What does John's visionary look into heaven reveal about the true nature of Christ?

_____

_____

_____

_____

_____

_____

7) If these are the awe-inspired actions of those with the clearest view of the Lord, how should we alter _our_ actions here and now?

_____

_____

_____

_____

_____

_____

8) Christ humbled himself by taking the form of a bondservant. What does it mean for you to have the heart of a servant?

_____

_____

_____

_____

_____

9) Jesus experienced suffering before glory, humiliation before exaltation. How does this truth differ from the modern, popular versions of the gospel espoused in many churches?

_____

_____

_____

_____

_____

_____

TRUTH FOR TODAY

The centrality to the gospel of the lordship of Jesus Christ is abundantly clear. In the New Testament, He is called Lord some 747 times. In the book of Acts, He is referred to as Savior only twice, but as Lord 92 times. The first known creed of the early church was "Jesus is Lord!" The lordship of Jesus Christ is the very essence of Christianity. Nowhere does Scripture speak of "making Jesus the Lord of your life." Many people who use that phrase are referring to believers' obedient submission to Jesus' sovereign authority. However, such expressions are seriously misleading and confusing. The problem is especially serious because some evangelicals maintain that confessing Jesus as Lord is not an integral part of saving faith. They wrongly view that as an optional, though desirable, step that believers should take sometime after they are saved. But it was God the Father who "made this Jesus . . . both Lord and Christ" (Acts 2:36 NKJV), and in order to be saved it is necessary for a person to "confess with [his] mouth the Lord Jesus" (Rom. 10:9 NKJV). Acknowledging Jesus as Lord must include submission and obedience, because, by definition, the title of Lord assumes it.

REFLECTING ON THE TEXT

10) Surrendering to the lordship of Christ will affect your priorities, values, and behavior. How would living under Christ's lordship change how you approach the following areas of your life?

⌐ Work/career

⌐ Family/home life

- Handling of money and possessions
- Stewardship of spiritual gifts, natural abilities, relationships, and opportunities

_____

_____

_____

_____

_____

_____

_____

_____

_____

11) What new insights have you gained into the true nature and glory of Christ? How will this alter your attitudes and actions this week?

_____

_____

_____

_____

_____

_____

_____

_____

_____

Personal Response

Write out additional reflections, questions you may have, or a prayer.

_____

_____

_____

_____

_____

_____

_____

_____

_____

_____

_____

_____

_____

_____

_____

_____

_____

_____

_____

_____

_____

_____

_____

_____

_____

6

GOD AT WORK IN YOU

Everyone has growth spurts unfortunately good times don't usually bring them on (handwritten)

DRAWING NEAR

Many Christians report "growth spurts" in their spiritual lives, when God has really worked in their lives. If you have had seasons of growth like this, indicate below when they were. What kind of life events or situations did God use to prompt this growth? (Example: a spiritual mentor, financial problems, physical illness, a Bible study group, becoming a parent, a shattering crisis, and so on.)

⁓ Childhood

⁓ Early adolescence

⁓ High-school years

⁓ College years

⁓ Young adulthood

⁓ Middle age

⁓ Empty nest

⁓ Golden years/retirement

THE CONTEXT

From the earliest days of the church, the relationship between the power of God and the responsibility of believers in living the Christian life has been debated. Is the Christian life essentially a matter of passive trust or of active obedience? Is it all God's doing, all the believer's doing, or a combination of both? This is not an unusual question when dealing with spiritual truth; in fact, the same question arises about salvation itself. Is it all God's doing, or is there a requirement on man's part in response to the command to believe the gospel? Scripture makes it clear that it involves both God's sovereignty and human response.

In Philippians 2:12–13, Paul presents the appropriate resolution between the believer's part and God's part in sanctification. Yet he makes no effort to rationally harmonize the two. He is content with the incomprehensibility and simply states both truths, saying, in effect, that on the one hand, sanctification is of believers, and on the other hand, it is of God.

KEYS TO THE TEXT

Work Out Your Salvation: The Greek verb rendered "work out" means "to continually work to bring something to fulfillment or completion." It cannot refer to salvation by works (see Rom. 3:21–24; Eph. 2:8–9), but it does refer to the believer's responsibility for active pursuit of obedience in the process of sanctification. The word *your* has the more emphatic meaning of "your own." The principle of working out salvation pertains to personal conduct, to faithful, obedient daily living. Such obedience obviously involves active commitment and personal effort. Sin in every form is to be renounced and put off and replaced by righteous thinking. Believers are to cleanse themselves "from all filthiness of the flesh and spirit, perfecting holiness in the fear of God" (2 Cor. 7:1 NKJV).

UNLEASHING THE TEXT

Read 2:12–13, noting the key words and definitions next to the passage.

obeyed (v. 12)—their faithful response to the divine commands Paul had taught them (see Rom. 1:5; 15:18; 2 Cor. 10:5–6)

fear and trembling (v. 12)—The attitude with which Christians are to pursue their sanctification. It involves a healthy fear of offending God and a righteous awe and respect for Him (see Prov. 1:7; 9:10; Isa. 66:1–2).

Philippians 2:12–13 (NKJV)

12 *Therefore, my beloved, as you have always obeyed, not as in my presence only, but now much more in my absence, work out your own salvation with fear and trembling;*

13 *for it is God who works in you both to will and to do for His good pleasure.*

God who works in you (v. 13)—Although the believer is responsible to work (v. 12), the Lord actually produces the good works and spiritual fruit in the lives of believers (John 15:5; 1 Cor. 12:6). This is accomplished because He works through us by His indwelling Spirit (Acts 1:8; 1 Cor. 3:16–17; 6:19–20; see Gal. 3:3).

you are not your own

start in Spirit end in flesh

God's temple

to will and to do (v. 13)—God energizes both the believer's desires and his actions. The Greek word for "will" indicates that He is not focusing on mere desires or whimsical emotions but on the studied intent to fulfill a planned purpose. God's power makes His church willing to live godly lives (see Ps. 110:3).

good pleasure (v. 13)—God wants Christians to do what satisfies Him (see Eph. 1:5, 9; 2 Thess. 1:11).

1) How would you answer a person who insisted that "work *out* your own salvation" means "work *for* your own salvation"?

2) According to Paul, what is to be our attitude as we work out our salvation? Why? *What is something you can relate to fear & awe*

Fred - electricity   me - Chemo drugs that cut to the bone.

or chemicals/drugs that will dissolve bones

Healthy fear - ocean
machinery
power of a car

3) Paul said that God is at work within believers. The verb used refers to being energized and active in a particular endeavor. What does this suggest about God's role in our growth?

49

4) What does Paul say here about God's will and our will?

_____

_____

_____

_____

_____

_____

5) What is the ultimate goal for cooperating with God's working in us (v. 13)? How does Ephesians 2:10 echo this idea?

Holiness !!!

_____

_____

_____

_____

_____

GOING DEEPER

Paul said that the Christian life is not passive, waiting for God to supernaturally and instantly transform us. For more on our part, read 1 Corinthians 9:24–27.

24 *Do you not know that those who run in a race all run, but one receives the prize? Run in such a way that you may obtain it.*

25 *And everyone who competes for the prize is temperate in all things. Now they do it to obtain a perishable crown, but we for an imperishable crown.*

26 *Therefore I run thus: not with uncertainty. Thus I fight: not as one who beats the air.*

27 *But I discipline my body and bring it into subjection, lest, when I have preached to others, I myself should become disqualified.*

Exploring the Meaning

6) What is the analogy or metaphor used by Paul in 1 Corinthians 9? How does this rigorous description of the Christian life square with your understanding and practice?

_____

_____

_____

_____

_____

7) There are two errors into which Christians may fall concerning the doctrine of sanctification, or becoming holy. On the one hand, we can stress God's role in sanctification, to the virtual exclusion of any human effort. On the other, we can emphasize self-effort at the expense of reliance on God's power. How does Philippians 2:12–13 solve this dilemma?

_____

_____

_____

_____

_____

_____

8) Why is divine initiative the prerequisite to holy resolve (see Ps. 27:8)? How does holy resolve lead to holy living?

_____

_____

_____

_____

_____

_____

Truth for Today

Salvation has three time dimensions: past, present, and future. The past dimension is that of *justification*, when believers placed their faith in Jesus Christ as Savior and Lord and were redeemed. The present dimension is *sanctification*, the time between a believer's justification and his death or the Rapture. The future aspect is *glorification*, when salvation is completed and believers receive their glorified bodies.

Holy living, then, demands that we commit our lives and energy to the service of Jesus Christ with every faculty we possess. Every command in Scripture would otherwise be meaningless. In fact, the first and great commandment calls for all-out effort: "You shall love the LORD your God with all your heart, with all your soul, with all your mind, and with all your strength" (Mark 12:30 NKJV). Believers must use all their energies in serving the Lord with diligence. At the same time, all that is accomplished within us is the work of God.

Reflecting on the Text

9) What would your life look like if your conscious commitment was to "work out your own salvation with fear and trembling"? How would your life be different?

_____

_____

_____

_____

_____

10) List several evidences that prove God is at work in you. (What changes have occurred in your life that are explainable only by your willing submission to the supernatural work of the Spirit?)

_____

_____

_____

_____

_____

Personal Response

Write out additional reflections, questions you may have, or a prayer.

Additional Notes

7

STOP COMPLAINING!

DRAWING NEAR

In this passage Paul talks about not complaining, but living blameless lives. Use the chart below to gauge how you typically respond to life's unpleasant situations. Put a check mark in all appropriate columns.

	Petty annoyances or irritations	Chronic, ongoing trials	Major crises or tragedies
Cry			
Curse			
Complain			
Pray			
Get angry or resentful			
Rejoice			
Seek some kind of escape			
Go into "denial mode"			
Determine to honor God			

THE CONTEXT

Modern Western society is the most prosperous culture in the history of mankind, and also arguably the most discontented society ever. As the economy has become increasingly richer, people appear more discontent and complain more with each passing generation. Fueling that enchantment is the conviction that personal happiness, though elusive and unattained, is the supreme objective of life.

The church is not immune to this. Believers' failure to willingly, even joyfully, submit to God's providential will is a deep-seated and serious sin. Discontentment and complaining are attitudes that can become so habitual they are hardly noticed. But those twin sins demonstrate a lack of trust in His providential will, boundless grace, and infinite wisdom and love. Consequently, those sins are especially odious in His sight and merit His discipline. To deal with the complainers in the Philippian congregation, Paul first commanded them to stop complaining, then gave them reasons for obeying that command.

KEYS TO THE TEXT

Without Complaining and Disputing: The Greek word for "complaining" is a term that actually sounds like what it means. Its pronunciation is much like muttering in a low tone of voice, like a grumbling sound. It is an emotional rejection of God's providence, will, and circumstances for one's life. The word for "disputing" is more intellectual and here means "questionings" or "criticisms" directed negatively toward God. This is a negative response to something unpleasant, inconvenient, or disappointing that one self-centeredly believes is undeserved. Whereas complaining is essentially emotional, disputing is essentially intellectual. A person who continues to murmur and grumble against God will eventually argue and dispute with Him.

UNLEASHING THE TEXT

Read 2:14–16, noting the key words and definitions next to the passage.

Philippians 2:14–16 (NKJV)

that you may become (v. 15)—This introduces the reasons believers should have the right attitude in pursuing godliness. "Become" indicates a process—they are to be growing toward something they do not yet fully possess as children of God (see Eph. 5:1; Tit. 2:1).

14 *Do all things without complaining and disputing,*
15 *that you may become blameless and harmless,*
    children of God without fault in the midst of a

blameless and harmless (v. 15)—"Blameless" describes a life that cannot be criticized because of sin or evil. "Harmless," which can also be translated "innocent," describes a life that is pure, unmixed, and unadulterated with sin, much like high-quality metal without any alloy (see Matt. 10:16; Rom. 16:19; 2 Cor. 11:3; Eph. 5:27).

without fault (v. 15)—This can also be translated "above reproach." In the Greek Old Testament, it is used several times of the kind of sacrifice to be brought to God, i.e., spotless and without blemish (see Num. 6:14; 19:2; 2 Pet. 3:14).

crooked and perverse generation (v. 15)—See Deuteronomy 32:5. *Crooked* is the word from which the English *scoliosis* (curvature of the spinal column) comes. It describes something that is deviated from the standard, which is true of all who stray from God's path (see Prov. 2:15; Isa. 53:6). *Perverse* intensifies this meaning by referring to one who has strayed so far off the path that his deviation is severely twisted and distorted (see Luke 9:41). Paul applies this condition to the sinful world system.

Is 59; 7 + 8

crooked and perverse generation, among whom you shine as lights in the world,

16 holding fast the word of life, so that I may rejoice in the day of Christ that I have not run in vain or labored in vain.

shine as lights (v. 15)—A metaphorical reference to spiritual character. The word *shine* can be more precisely rendered "you have to shine," which means believers must show their character in the midst of a dark culture, as the sun, moon, and stars shine in an otherwise dark sky (see Matt. 5:14; 2 Cor. 4:6; Eph. 5:8).

holding fast (v. 16)—A slightly different translation—"holding forth"—more accurately reflects the verb in the original text. Here it refers to believers' holding out or offering something for others to take.

the word of life (v. 16)—the gospel which, when believed, produces spiritual and eternal life (see Eph. 2:1)

run ... or labored in vain (v. 16)—Paul wanted to look back on his ministry and see that all his efforts were worthwhile.

[handwritten: II Tim 2:2 3 Tit 3:9]

1) Define what Paul means by "complaining and disputing."

[handwritten, left margin: Books]

[handwritten: Complaining has an element of self justification I shouldn't have to because]

[handwritten: disputing - question the validity (motive) Verbal controversy arguing - state reasons for & against]

2) Why was it so important for the Philippians to live a life free of complaining and disputing? What difference does the absence of such behavior make? What was at stake?

[handwritten: emotional rejection + intellectual rejection of one's position is complete rejection]

[handwritten: @ stake - You put yourself in God's position or place your relationship with God]

3) How did Paul describe the world in which the Philippians lived?

[handwritten: Crooked & perverse deviated from the standard   so far off deviation is even twisted   gateway to greater sin → greater sin]

57

4) How does a lifestyle of grumbling violate Paul's command to be blameless and without fault?

grumble - Not addressing in open - stirs up dissention

Wholehearted unmixed devotion to doing God's will — No longer willing obedience

5) Instead of grumbling and arguing with God about their lot in life, Paul urged the Philippians to remember their mission. What exactly was their calling (vv. 15–16)?

shine like stars
hold out word of truth
endorsing what you believe in

People silent before God _Lev 10_ _Aaron- sons killed_
Elijah- stomped up mtn Job -
Hab 2:20

GOING DEEPER

Those who know Christ are called to a radically different lifestyle. We are to see the world from a new perspective, evaluate situations with renewed minds, talk and act and react in new, God-honoring ways. Read 1 Peter 2:9–17.

9 *But you are a chosen generation, a royal priesthood, a holy nation, His own special people, that you may proclaim the praises of Him who called you out of darkness into His marvelous light;*

10 *who once were not a people but are now the people of God, who had not obtained mercy but now have obtained mercy.*

11 *Beloved, I beg you as sojourners and pilgrims, abstain from fleshly lusts which war against the soul,*

12 *having your conduct honorable among the Gentiles, that when they speak against you as evildoers, they may, by your good works which they observe, glorify God in the day of visitation.*

13 *Therefore submit yourselves to every ordinance of man for the Lord's sake, whether to the king as supreme,*

14 *or to governors, as to those who are sent by him for the punishment of evildoers and for the praise of those who do good.*

15 *For this is the will of God, that by doing good you may put to silence the ignorance of foolish men—*

16 *as free, yet not using liberty as a cloak for vice, but as bondservants of God.*

17 *Honor all people. Love the brotherhood. Fear God. Honor the king.*

EXPLORING THE MEANING

6) What parallels do you see between the exhortation in Philippians 2:14–16 and the charge in 1 Peter 2:9–17?

_____

_____

_____

_____

7) Is there ever a time in which it is appropriate to grumble or argue with God? Why? When we do question or doubt God's goodness or power, what are the consequences?

_____

_____

_____

_____

8) How does one replace the habit of doubt and grumbling with a habit of dependence and gratitude?

_____

_____

_____

_____

TRUTH FOR TODAY

Every circumstance of life is to be accepted willingly and joyfully, without murmuring, complaint, or disappointment, much less resentment. There is no exception. There should never be either emotional grumbling or intellectual disputing. It is always sinful for believers to complain about anything the Lord calls them to do or about any circumstance which He sovereignly allows. Whether the task is difficult or easy, whether the situation involves a blessing or a trial, negative attitudes are forbidden. As he testifies later in this letter, Paul's own spiritual growth had led him to enjoy this attitude: "I have learned in whatever state I am, to be content: I know how to be abased, and I know how to abound. Everywhere and in all things I have learned both to be full and to be hungry, both to abound and to suffer need" (Phil. 4:11–12 NKJV). His example shows that such righteous behavior is possible. *beatings, shipwrecks, prison, trials, flogging left for dead*

REFLECTING ON THE TEXT

9) In what specific situations today do you need to make a concerted effort not to grumble or question God's dealings? What is your plan for putting to death the habit of complaining?

_____

_____

_____

_____

10) What does it mean to "shine" for Christ? List some specific qualities that make a believer's life sparkle and stand out against a culture shrouded in spiritual darkness.

_____

_____

_____

_____

_____

_____

11) What are some specific ways you can "hold forth" the Word of truth to others this week?

_____

_____

_____

_____

_____

PERSONAL RESPONSE

Write out additional reflections, questions you may have, or a prayer.

_____

_____

_____

_____

_____

_____

_____

_____

_____

_____

_____

_____

_____

_____

_____

_____

ADDITIONAL NOTES

8

MODEL SPIRITUAL SERVANTS

DRAWING NEAR

Compose a personal servanthood "résumé." Since becoming a follower of Christ and a member of a church, what are some ministry roles you've filled? Which of those have you enjoyed most? Least?

_____

_____

_____

_____

_____

_____

_____

THE CONTEXT

The seventeenth-century Puritan Thomas Brooks wisely observed, "Example is the most powerful rhetoric." Philippians 2:17–30 presents three men whose lives are exceptional patterns for godly living. Paul, Timothy, and Epaphroditus were together in Rome at this time. Paul was a prisoner in his own rented quarters. Though chained to a soldier, he was free to carry on his work unhindered. Timothy, the apostle's son in the faith, had been with him for some time. Epaphroditus had been sent from the Philippian church to bring financial support for Paul and to minister to his needs. The men were knit together geographically, spiritually, and ministerially in a common cause. Each was passionately devoted to the Lord Jesus Christ, not consumed with his own interests. For the Lord's sake, each had risked his health, his freedom, and even his life.

KEYS TO THE TEXT

Drink Offering: This refers to the topping off of an ancient animal sacrifice. The priest poured wine either in front or on top of the burning animal, and the wine would vaporize. That steam symbolized the rising of the offering to the deity for whom the sacrifice was made (see Ex. 29:38–41; 2 Kings 16:13). Paul viewed his entire life as a drink offering, and here it was poured out on the Philippians' sacrificial service.

Epaphroditus: A native Philippian of whom, outside this passage, little is known. His name was common in Greek, taken from a familiar word that originally meant "favorite of Aphrodite" (Greek goddess of love). Later, the name came to mean "lovely" or "loving." He was sent to Paul with gifts (4:18) and was to remain with and serve Paul as he could (v. 30).

Unleashing the Text

Read 2:17–30, noting the key words and definitions next to the passage.

Philippians 2:17–30 (NKJV)

I . . . rejoice . . . you also . . . rejoice (vv. 17, 18)—An attitude of mutual joy ought to accompany any sacrificial Christian service (see 2 Cor. 7:4; Col. 1:24; 1 Thess. 3:9).

being poured out (v. 17)—From the Greek it means "to be offered as a libation or drink offering." Some connect this with Paul's future martyrdom, but the verb is in the present tense, which means he is referring to his sacrificial ministry among the Philippians.

service of your faith (v. 17)—"Service" comes from a word that refers to sacred, priestly service (see Rom. 12:1; 1 Cor. 9:12) and was so used in the Greek Old Testament. Paul sees the Philippians as priests who were offering their lives sacrificially and faithfully in service to God (see 1 Pet. 2:9).

17 Yes, and if I am being poured out as a drink offering on the sacrifice and service of your faith, I am glad and rejoice with you all.
18 For the same reason you also be glad and rejoice with me.
19 But I trust in the Lord Jesus to send Timothy to you shortly, that I also may be encouraged when I know your state.
20 For I have no one like-minded, who will sincerely care for your state.
21 For all seek their own, not the things which are of Christ Jesus.
22 But you know his proven character, that as a son with his father he served with me in the gospel.
23 Therefore I hope to send him at once, as soon as I see how it goes with me.
24 But I trust in the Lord that I myself shall also come shortly.

I have no one like-minded (v. 20)—Literally, "one souled," and often translated "kindred spirit." Timothy was one in thought, feeling, and spirit with Paul in his love for the church. He was unique, as he was Paul's protégé (see 1 Tim. 1:2; 2 Tim. 1:2). Paul had no other friend like Timothy because, sadly, "all" the others were devoted to their own purposes rather than Christ's.

in the Lord (v. 24)—Paul knew his plans were subject to God's sovereignty (see James 4:13–17).

25 *Yet I considered it necessary to send to you Epaphroditus, my brother, fellow worker, and fellow soldier, but your messenger and the one who ministered to my need;*

26 *since he was longing for you all, and was distressed because you had heard that he was sick.*

27 *For indeed he was sick almost unto death; but God had mercy on him, and not only on him but on me also, lest I should have sorrow upon sorrow.*

28 *Therefore I sent him the more eagerly, that when you see him again you may rejoice, and I may be less sorrowful.*

29 *Receive him therefore in the Lord with all gladness, and hold such men in esteem;*

30 *because for the work of Christ he came close to death, not regarding his life, to supply what was lacking in your service toward me.*

messenger (v. 25)—This comes from the same word that yields the English *apostle*. He was not an apostle of Christ, but an apostle ("sent one"), in the broader sense, of the church in Philippi, sent to Paul with their monetary love gift (see 2 Cor. 8:23). Paul needed to explain why he sent him back to the church with this letter, lest they think Epaphroditus had not served Paul well.

distressed (v. 26)—The Greek term describes the confused, chaotic, heavy state of restlessness that results from a time of turmoil or great trauma. Epaphroditus was more concerned about the Philippians' worry for him than he was about his own difficult situation.

sick almost unto death (v. 27)— It is possible that by the time Epaphroditus arrived in Rome, he had become seriously ill, but now he was recovered enough to go back home to labor with the church, who needed him more than Paul did.

sorrowful (v. 28)—This is more accurately translated "concern" or "anxiety." Paul had a great burden for all the people in the churches (see 2 Cor. 11:2), and he was concerned here because the Philippians were so distressed about Epaphroditus.

esteem (v. 29)—Men like him are worthy of honor.

close to death (v. 30)—This refers to the same thing mentioned as sickness in vv. 26–27.

1) How did Paul describe his life and ministry (v. 17)? To what is he referring in these phrases?

_____

_____

_____

_____

_____

_____

_____

_____

2) What qualities did Timothy exhibit that made him such a model servant?

_____

_____

_____

_____

_____

3) How did Paul describe the character of Epaphroditus?

_____

_____

_____

_____

4) What happened to Epaphroditus, and what was his unusual response?

_____

_____

_____

_____

_____

5) What were Paul's instructions to the church at Philippi regarding how to treat men like Epaphroditus?

_____

_____

_____

_____

_____

_____

Going Deeper

God's primary tools for changing lives are the Word of God and the Spirit of God. Paul's relationship with Timothy shows that God also uses people to make a difference in others' lives. Read 1 Thessalonians 3:1–10.

1 *Therefore, when we could no longer endure it, we thought it good to be left in Athens alone,*

2 *and sent Timothy, our brother and minister of God, and our fellow laborer in the gospel of Christ, to establish you and encourage you concerning your faith,*

3 *that no one should be shaken by these afflictions; for you yourselves know that we are appointed to this.*

4 *For, in fact, we told you before when we were with you that we would suffer tribulation, just as it happened, and you know.*

5 *For this reason, when I could no longer endure it, I sent to know your faith, lest by some means the tempter had tempted you, and our labor might be in vain.*

6 *But now that Timothy has come to us from you, and brought us good news of your faith and love, and that you always have good remembrance of us, greatly desiring to see us, as we also to see you—*

7 *therefore, brethren, in all our affliction and distress we were comforted concerning you by your faith.*

8 *For now we live, if you stand fast in the Lord.*

9 *For what thanks can we render to God for you, for all the joy with which we rejoice for your sake before our God,*

10 *night and day praying exceedingly that we may see your face and perfect what is lacking in your faith?*

Exploring the Meaning

6) What does this passage from 1 Thessalonians reveal about the inner workings of the early church and the healthy exercise of ministry?

_____

_____

_____

_____

_____

7) Timothy followed Paul's example of service. Do you have a spiritual mentor, a "Paul," whom you learn from and serve with? Who is your "Timothy"?

_____

_____

_____

_____

_____

_____

8) What are some qualities in Epaphroditus's life that you'd like to emulate?

_____

_____

_____

Truth for Today

Selfless service for Christ is a sacrifice only in the sense of being an offering to God. It is never a sacrifice in the sense of being a loss. A believer can sacrifice nothing for the Lord that is not replaced with something infinitely more valuable and gratifying (2 Cor. 4:17). It is always an exchange of the lesser for the greater. What he forsook was mere "rubbish"; what he gained was Christ and the immeasurable blessings of salvation and eternal life (Phil. 3:8–11). The reason many believers know little about Paul's kind of joy is that they know little about his kind of sacrifice.

Reflecting on the Text

9) Genuine, biblical love always requires personal sacrifice. In what specific ways are you sacrificing out of love for God or love for others?

_____

_____

_____

10) List two practical ways you can show appreciation to the servant-leaders who have marked your life in profound ways. Put them into practice this week.

_____

_____

_____

_____

11) The common denominator among Paul, Timothy, and Epaphroditus was a wholesale surrender to the purposes of God, marked by a selfless, servant spirit. What can you do to become this kind of Christian worker?

_____

_____

_____

_____

_____

_____

PERSONAL RESPONSE

Write out additional reflections, questions you may have, or a prayer.

_____

_____

_____

_____

_____

_____

_____

_____

Additional Notes

9

THE DISTINGUISHING MARKS
OF TRUE BELIEVERS

DRAWING NEAR

The Bible insists there is a huge difference in the behavior of believers and that of "make-believers." How can we tell we are truly saved?

Ask about Next study. Matthew ?

THE CONTEXT

The good news of forgiveness and eternal life is the heart of the New Testament message. But it also challenges professing believers to examine themselves and make certain their faith is genuine. In Philippians 3:1–3, Paul adds to the biblical teaching of distinguishing between genuine and false faith. Both implicitly and explicitly, he presents five qualities of true believers: they rejoice in the Lord, exercise discernment, worship in the Spirit, glory in Christ Jesus, and put no confidence in the flesh.

This autobiographical passage introduces Paul's dramatic and compelling salvation testimony. It is also one of the most significant statements of the doctrine of salvation in Scripture, revealing the internal work of God in a truly repentant and believing sinner.

KEYS TO THE TEXT

Rubbish: This very strong word can also be rendered "waste," "dung," "manure," or even "excrement." Paul expresses in the strongest possible language his utter disdain for all the religious credits with which he had sought to impress man and God. In view of the surpassing value of knowing Christ, they are worthless. Paul would have heartily endorsed Isaiah's declaration, "We are all like an unclean thing, and all our righteousnesses are like filthy rags; we all fade as a leaf, and our iniquities, like the wind, have taken us away" (Isa. 64:6 NKJV).

Unleashing the Text

Read 3:1–11, noting the key words and definitions next to the passage.

Philippians 3:1–11 (NKJV)

Finally (v. 1)—Paul has reached a transition point—but not a conclusion, since 44 verses remain (see 4:8).

1 *Finally, my brethren, rejoice in the Lord. For me to write the same things to you is not tedious, but for you it is safe.*

rejoice in the Lord (v. 1)— Paul's familiar theme throughout the epistle; this, however, is the first time he adds "in the Lord," which signifies the sphere in which the believers' joy exists—a sphere unrelated to the circumstances of life, but related to an unassailable, unchanging relationship to the sovereign Lord.

2 *Beware of dogs, beware of evil workers, beware of the mutilation!*

3 *For we are the circumcision, who worship God in the Spirit, rejoice in Christ Jesus, and have no confidence in the flesh,*

4 *though I also might have confidence in the flesh. If anyone else thinks he may have confidence in the flesh, I more so:*

dogs (v. 2)—During the first century, dogs roamed the streets

5 *circumcised the eighth day, of the stock of Israel, of*

and were essentially wild scavengers. Because dogs were such filthy animals, the Jews loved to refer to Gentiles as dogs. Yet here Paul refers to Jews, specifically the Judaizers, as dogs, to describe their sinful, vicious, and uncontrolled character.

evil workers (v. 2)—The Judaizers prided themselves on being workers of righteousness. Yet Paul described their works as evil, since any attempt to please God by one's own efforts and draw attention away from Christ's accomplished redemption is the worst kind of wickedness.

mutilation (v. 2)—In contrast to the Greek word for "circumcision," which means "to cut around," this term means "to cut down (off)." The Judaizers' circumcision was, ironically, no spiritual symbol; it was merely physical mutilation.

we are the circumcision (v. 3)—The true people of God do not possess merely a symbol of the need for a clean heart; they actually have been cleansed of sin by God.

worship God in the Spirit (v. 3)—This is the first characteristic Paul uses to define a true believer. The Greek word for "worship" means to render respectful spiritual service, while "Spirit" should have a small *s*, to indicate the inner person.

no confidence in the flesh (v. 3)—By "flesh" Paul is referring to man's unredeemed humanness, his own ability and achievements apart from God. The Jews placed their confidence in being circumcised, being descendants of Abraham, and performing the external ceremonies and duties of the Mosaic law—things that could not save them. The true believer views his flesh as sinful, without any capacity to merit salvation or please God.

the eighth day (v. 5)—Paul was circumcised on the prescribed day (Gen. 17:12; 21:4; Lev. 12:3).

of Israel (v. 5)—All true Jews were direct descendants of Abraham, Isaac, and Jacob (Israel). Paul's Jewish heritage was pure.

the tribe of Benjamin, a Hebrew of the Hebrews; concerning the law, a Pharisee;

6 concerning zeal, persecuting the church; concerning the righteousness which is in the law, blameless.

7 But what things were gain to me, these I have counted loss for Christ.

8 Yet indeed I also count all things loss for the excellence of the knowledge of Christ Jesus my Lord, for whom I have suffered the loss of all things, and count them as rubbish, that I may gain Christ

9 and be found in Him, not having my own righteousness, which is from the law, but that which is through faith in Christ, the righteousness which is from God by faith;

10 that I may know Him and the power of His

of the tribe of Benjamin (v. 5)—Benjamin was the second son of Rachel (Gen. 35:18) and one of the elite tribes of Israel, who, along with Judah, remained loyal to the Davidic dynasty and formed the southern kingdom (1 Kings 12:21).

Hebrew of the Hebrews (v. 5)—Paul was born to Hebrew parents and maintained the Hebrew tradition and language, even while living in a pagan city (see Acts 21:40; 26:4–5).

a Pharisee (v. 5)—the legalistic fundamentalists of Judaism, whose zeal to apply the Old Testament Scriptures directly to life led to a complex system of tradition and works righteousness

zeal, persecuting the church (v. 6)—To the Jew, "zeal" was the highest single virtue of religion. It combines love and hate; because Paul loved Judaism, he hated whatever might threaten it.

the righteousness which is in the law (v. 6)—The standard of righteous living advocated by God's law. Paul outwardly kept this, so that no one could accuse him of violation. Obviously his heart was sinful and self-righteous. He was not an Old Testament believer, but a proud and lost legalist.

what things were gain . . . I have counted loss (v. 7)—The Greek word for "gain" is an accounting term that means "profit." The Greek word for "loss" also is an accounting term, used to describe a business loss. Paul used the language of business to describe the spiritual transaction that occurred when Christ redeemed him. All his Jewish religious credentials that he thought were in his profit column, were actually worthless and damning. Thus, he put them in his loss column when he saw the glories of Christ (see Matt. 13:44, 45; 16:25, 26).

knowledge of Christ Jesus (v. 8)—To "know" Christ is not simply to have intellectual knowledge about Him; Paul used the Greek verb that means to know "experientially" or "personally" (see John 10:27; 17:3; 2 Cor. 4:6; 1 John 5:20). It is equivalent to shared life with Christ. It also corresponds to a Hebrew word used of God's knowledge of His people (Amos 3:2) and their knowledge of Him in love and obedience (Jer. 31:34; Hos. 6:3; 8:2).

be found in Him (v. 9)—Paul's union with Christ was possible only because God imputed Christ's righteousness to him so that it was reckoned by God as his own.

not having my own righteousness . . . from the law (v. 9)—This is the proud self-righteousness of external morality, religious ritual and ceremony, and good works. It is the righteousness produced by the flesh, which cannot save from sin (Rom. 3:19, 20; Gal. 3:6–25).

faith in Christ (v. 9)—Faith is the confident, continuous confession of total dependence on Jesus Christ as the necessary requirement to enter God's kingdom. And that requirement is the righteousness of Christ, which God imputes to every believer.

I may know Him (v. 10)—Paul's emphasis here is on gaining a deeper knowledge and intimacy with Christ.

the power of His resurrection (v. 10)—Christ's resurrection most graphically demonstrated the extent of His power. By raising Himself from the dead, Christ displayed His power over both the physical and spiritual worlds.

fellowship of His sufferings (v. 10)—This refers to a partnership—a deep communion of suffering that every believer shares with Christ, who is able to comfort suffering Christians because He has already experienced the same suffering, and infinitely more (Heb. 2:18; 4:15; 12:2–4; see 2 Cor. 5:21; 1 Pet. 2:21–24).

resurrection, and the fellowship of His sufferings, being conformed to His death,

11 *if, by any means, I may attain to the resurrection from the dead.*

conformed to His death (v. 10)—As Christ died for the purpose of redeeming sinners, so Paul had that same purpose in a lesser sense; he lived and would willingly die to reach sinners with the gospel. His life and death, though not redemptive, were for the same purpose as his Lord's.

by any means (v. 11)—Reflecting his humility, he didn't care how God brought it to pass, but longed for death and for the fulfillment of his salvation in his resurrection body (see Rom. 8:23).

the resurrection from the dead (v. 11)—Literally, "the resurrection out from the corpses." This is a reference to the resurrection that accompanies the rapture of the Church (1 Thess. 4:13–17; see 1 Cor. 15:42–44).

Who are Judaizers Today?

1) What was Paul's warning to the Philippians (v. 2)? To whom was he referring?

Judaizers - sinful, vicious + uncontrolled

People who have knowledge of God but their heart is not about leading others to God but ripping others up using the law Using the letter of the law - totally disregarding what the intent was - think nazi - ss

2) In verses 2 and 3, Paul speaks of a circumcision that transcends the physical realm. How did he describe this "true" circumcision?

Trusting not in themselves + their rightness - heritage - etc.

(Circumcision - changing the appearance of their lives)

3) What were the high points of Paul's "religious résumé"? (vv. 4–6)

① Pure Jew, ② circumcised on the right day ③ Knew the law ④ practiced it without flaw on the outside ⑤ Zeal - love / hate of God + what was for/against Him

4) In the heart of the passage, Paul uses accounting terminology (vv. 7–8). How do these terms explain spiritual realities?

Those things that would give human credentials are a loss if you count on them instead of counting on what God requires

5) What prompted Paul to view his former credentials as rubbish?

He knew His heart was not pure before God because of His credentials. We have to know id we can't earn right standing in God's eyes. He requires a life to pay for any infraction of His law. Blood must cover sin to pay the price

Going Deeper

Many people think salvation is a reward for the person who lives a moral, upstanding life. And yet, as Paul discovered, the amazing grace of God is the only way to reconciliation with God. See another vivid illustration of this in Luke 18:9–14.

9   *Also He spoke this parable to some who trusted in themselves that they were righteous, and despised others:*

10 *"Two men went up to the temple to pray, one a Pharisee and the other a tax collector.*

11 *The Pharisee stood and prayed thus with himself, 'God, I thank You that I am not like other men—extortioners, unjust, adulterers, or even as this tax collector.*

12 *I fast twice a week; I give tithes of all that I possess.'*

13 *And the tax collector, standing afar off, would not so much as raise his eyes to heaven, but beat his breast, saying, 'God, be merciful to me a sinner!'*

14 *I tell you, this man went down to his house justified rather than the other; for everyone who exalts himself will be humbled, and he who humbles himself will be exalted."*

Exploring the Meaning

6) How does Paul's life mirror the experiences of both of the men described in Luke 18:9–14?

Paul was the first man. He trusted
in outward appearance of righteousness
instead of God's Grace

2nd man is Paul after He comes to know
Christ, He understands there is no
way to earn right standing in God's "eyes"

7) List some of the dramatic ways Paul's goals and motives changed after coming to know Christ?

He doesn't trust in his own accomplishments He is willing to give up his own life to bring others to Christ

8) What are some ways the gospel of grace gets overshadowed by an emphasis on human effort and religious "performance" at your church? In your own life?

9) How do Paul's words in Philippians 3:1–11 demonstrate the old saying that Christianity is not a religion but a *relationship* with Christ?

Your faith needs to be in an inner trust + dependence on God's mercy not a list of do's + don'ts + how well you can keep them

TRUTH FOR TODAY

Many people rest their hope of salvation on a past event. They may have prayed to receive Christ as a child, gone forward in response to an altar call, signed a card, or made a commitment at a retreat. Sometimes well-meaning people encourage such false hopes by offering a seemingly plausible syllogism to those who pray to receive Christ: "John 1:12 says that 'as many as received Him, to them He gave the right to become children of God, to those who believe in His name'; you just received Christ; therefore you have become a child of God." Unfortunately, that syllogism is only true if the minor premise ("you just received Christ") is true. And that is the very point in question. Genuine faith will inevitably produce transformation in a person's life; false or dead faith will not (see James 2:14–26). Scripture nowhere points people back to a conversion experience to validate their salvation; the issue is a changed life. *Nazarite vow hair cut + burned after vow completed / no trophies of past experiences*

REFLECTING ON THE TEXT

10) The apostle Paul met Christ on the Damascus Road (see Acts 9:1–31) in about AD 33–34. Why then, three decades later at this writing, would he express the hope "that I may know Him"? Didn't he already know Christ by that time?

Know experientialy - Continuous Knowing not like a friend you used to know

11) How does Paul's passion for Christ challenge you today? What needs to change in your life?

12) What distinguishing marks of true faith are present in your life? What signs are missing?

_____

_____

_____

_____

_____

PERSONAL RESPONSE

Write out additional reflections, questions you may have, or a prayer.

_____

_____

_____

_____

_____

_____

_____

_____

_____

_____

_____

_____

_____

ADDITIONAL NOTES

10

REACHING FOR THE PRIZE

DRAWING NEAR

Faith can be compared to a long-term race. Were you ever involved in athletics? If so, what were some lessons you learned by participating in and/or watching your favorite sport?

_____

_____

_____

_____

_____

THE CONTEXT

Judging from the frequent use of athletic metaphors in his writings, the apostle Paul must have been a sports fan. He made reference to boxing, wrestling, and the Isthmian games (1 Cor. 9:25–26; Eph. 6:12). Paul's favorite athletic imagery was that of a footrace (Acts 20:24; Rom. 9:16; 1 Cor. 9:24; 2 Tim. 4:7), and it is this metaphor of the Christian life that is the theme of this passage. Here we see Paul's passionate concern for spiritual growth.

Having heard Paul's remarkable testimony of transformation, some people in Philippi might have mistakenly assumed that Paul had reached spiritual perfection. But Paul was still subject to temptation, still possessed his unredeemed flesh, and was still a sinner. Far from having obtained perfection, he was pursuing it with all his might. Paul understood that the Christian life is a lifelong process of "grow[ing] in the grace and knowledge of our Lord and Savior Jesus Christ" (2 Peter 3:18 NKJV).

KEYS TO THE TEXT

Press On: This phrase is from the Greek verb _dioko,_ which means "to pursue," or in some contexts "to persecute," or methodically oppress and harass a person or group. It has the extended connotation of pursuing a person on foot in a chase. From this latter image of the chase, it also conveys a sense of striving and pressing on to a goal with relentless intensity. The word was used to describe a sprinter, and thus refers to aggressive, energetic action. Paul pursued sanctification with all his might, straining every spiritual muscle to win the prize. Other believers should be quick to follow this apostolic example.

UNLEASHING THE TEXT

Read 3:12–21, noting the key words and definitions next to the passage.

Philippians 3:12–21 (NKJV)

Not that I have already attained (v. 12)—The race toward Christlikeness begins with a sense of dissatisfaction and honesty.

lay hold . . . laid hold of me (v. 12)— "Lay hold" means "to make one's own possession." Christ chose Paul for the ultimate purpose of conforming Paul to His glorious image (Rom. 8:29), and that is the very goal Paul pursued to attain.

apprehended (v. 13)—the same Greek word translated "laid hold" in v. 12

12 *Not that I have already attained, or am already perfected; but I press on, that I may lay hold of that for which Christ Jesus has also laid hold of me.*

13 *Brethren, I do not count myself to have apprehended; but one thing I do, forgetting those things which are behind and reaching forward to those things which are ahead,*

14 *I press toward the goal for the prize of the upward call of God in Christ Jesus.*

15 *Therefore let us, as many as are mature, have this mind; and if in anything you think otherwise, God will reveal even this to you.*

one thing I do (v. 13)—Paul had reduced the whole of sanctification to the simple and clear goal of doing "one thing"—pursuing Christlikeness.

forgetting . . . which are behind (v. 13)—The believer must refuse to rely on past virtuous deeds and achievements in ministry or to dwell on sins and failures. To be distracted by the past debilitates one's efforts in the present. *Num 36:5, 18   Philp 3:4-6*

the goal (v. 14)—Christlikeness here and now

the prize (v. 14)—Christlikeness in heaven (see vv. 20–21; 1 John 3:1–2)

the upward call of God (v. 14)—The time when God calls each believer up to heaven and into His presence will be the moment of receiving the prize, which has been an unattainable goal in earthly life.

as many as are mature (v. 15)—Since the spiritual perfection of Christlikeness is possible only when the believer receives the upward call, Paul is referring here to mature spirituality. He could be referring to the mature believers who were like-minded with him in this pursuit, or he may also have used "mature" here to refer sarcastically to the Judaizers, who thought they had reached perfection.

have this mind (v. 15)—A better translation is "attitude." Believers are to have the attitude of pursuing the prize of Christlikeness.

if . . . you think otherwise (v. 15)—those who continue to dwell on the past and make no progress toward the goal

God will reveal (v. 15)—The Greek word for "reveal" means "to uncover" or "unveil." Paul left in God's hands those who were not pursuing spiritual perfection. He knew God would reveal the truth to them eventually, even if it meant chastening (Heb. 12:5–11).

16 *Nevertheless, to the degree that we have already attained, let us walk by the same rule, let us be of the same mind.*

17 *Brethren, join in following my example, and note those who so walk, as you have us for a pattern.*

18 *For many walk, of whom I have told you often, and now tell you even weeping, that they are the enemies of the cross of Christ:*

19 *whose end is destruction, whose god is their belly, and whose glory is in their shame— who set their mind on earthly things.*

20 *For our citizenship is in heaven, from which we also eagerly wait for the Savior, the Lord Jesus Christ,*

to the degree . . . already attained, let us walk (v. 16)—The Greek word for "walk" refers to walking in line. Paul's directive for the Philippian believers was to stay in line spiritually and keep progressing in sanctification by the same principles that had brought them to this point in their spiritual growth (see 1 Thess. 3:10; 1 Pet. 2:2).

my example (v. 17)—Literally, "be imitators of me." Since all believers are imperfect, they need examples of less imperfect people who know how to deal with imperfection and who can model the process of pursuing the goal of Christlikeness. Paul was that model (1 Cor. 11:1; 1 Thess. 1:6).

note those who so walk (v. 17)—The Philippian believers were to follow the rule of godly examples such as Timothy and Epaphroditus (2:19–20), and see how they conducted themselves in service to Christ.

told you often (v. 18)—Apparently Paul had warned the Philippians on numerous occasions about the dangers of false teachers, just as he did the Ephesians (Acts 20:28–30).

weeping (v. 18)—Paul had a similar response as he warned the Ephesian elders about the dangers of false teachers (Acts 20:31).

enemies of the cross (v. 18)—Implied in Paul's language is that these men did not claim to oppose Christ, His work on the cross, or salvation by grace alone through faith alone; even so, they did not pursue Christlikeness in manifest godliness. Apparently, they were posing as friends of Christ, and possibly had even reached positions of leadership in the church.

end is destruction (v. 19)—The Greek word for "end" refers to one's ultimate destiny. The Judaizers were headed for eternal damnation because they depended on their works to save them. The Gentile libertines were headed for the same destiny because they trusted in their human wisdom and denied the transforming power of the gospel.

god . . . belly (v. 19)—This may refer to the Judaizers' fleshly accomplishments, which were mainly religious works. It could also refer to their observance of the dietary laws they believed were necessary for salvation. If the Gentile libertines are in view, it could easily refer to their sensual desires and fleshly appetites. As always, false teachers are evident by their wickedness.

glory . . . shame (v. 19)—The Judaizers boasted of their self-effort; but even the best of their accomplishments were no better than filthy rags or dung (vv. 7–8; Isa. 64:6). The Gentile libertines boasted about their sin and abused Christian liberty to defend their behavior (1 Cor. 6:12).

earthly things (v. 19)—The Judaizers were preoccupied with ceremonies, feasts, sacrifices, and other kinds of physical observances. The Gentile libertines simply loved the world itself and all the things in it (see James 4:4; 1 John 2:15).

our citizenship (v. 20)—The Greek term refers to a colony of foreigners. In one secular source, it was used to describe a capital city that kept the names of its citizens on a register.

in heaven (v. 20)—The place where God dwells and where Christ is present. It is the believers' home (John 14:2–3), where their names are registered (Luke 10:20) and their inheritance awaits (1 Pet. 1:4). Other believers are there (Heb. 12:23). We belong to the kingdom under the rule of our heavenly King, and obey heaven's laws (see 1 Pet. 2:11).

eagerly wait (v. 20)—The Greek verb is found in most passages dealing with the second coming and expresses the idea of waiting patiently, but with great expectation (Rom. 8:23; 2 Pet. 3:11–12).

transform our lowly body (v. 21)—The Greek word for "transform" gives us the word *schematic*, which is an internal design of something. Those who are already dead in Christ, but alive with Him in spirit in heaven (1:23; 2 Cor. 5:8; Heb. 12:23), will receive new bodies at the resurrection and rapture of the church, when those alive on earth will have their bodies transformed.

21 *who will transform our lowly body that it may be conformed to His glorious body, according to the working by which He is able even to subdue all things to Himself.*

conformed to His glorious body (v. 21)—The believer's new body will be like Christ's after His resurrection and will be redesigned and adapted for heaven (1 Cor. 15:42–43; 1 John 3:2).

subdue (v. 21)—The Greek word means "to subject" and refers to arranging things in order of rank or managing something. Christ has the power both to providentially create natural laws and miraculously overrule them (1 Cor. 15:23–27).

1) How did Paul vividly describe his rigorous and disciplined process of pursuing Christlikeness?

Like an athlete

2) What attitude was Paul advocating in verse 15?

attitude - Not I haven't arrived or I'll never get there

Do athletes say I wish I hadn't trained when they don't win or recognize the benefit

3) What command did Paul give the Philippians in verse 17? What does this suggest about the role that others should play in our spiritual growth?

We are not created to be alone but in relationships. Relationships help keep us balanced - show us many ways to accomplish goals. As Iron sharpeneth iron
prov 27:17

4) To whom was Paul referring by the term "enemies of the cross" (v. 18)? What behaviors marked their lives and ministries?

not necessarily unbelievers but discounting the power of God in lives - the power of His sacrifice posing as friends of Christ maybe even church leaders Judiazers - work of flesh Libertines - go ahead & sin God will forgive

5) How did Paul describe the true identity and ultimate destiny of believers in verses 19–21?

believing we are citizens of heaven

eagerly await a savior from there

~~God is stomach deeds or desir~~
Believe By power will bring everything under control - right priorities

Going Deeper

God is in the process of transforming us, and our "ultimate makeover" (spiritual and physical) still awaits us. Read 1 Corinthians 15:35–58; then continue to work through the questions below.

35 *But someone will say, "How are the dead raised up? And with what body do they come?"*

36 *Foolish one, what you sow is not made alive unless it dies.*

37 *And what you sow, you do not sow that body that shall be, but mere grain—perhaps wheat or some other grain.*

38 *But God gives it a body as He pleases, and to each seed its own body.*

39 *All flesh is not the same flesh, but there is one kind of flesh of men, another flesh of animals, another of fish, and another of birds.*

40 *There are also celestial bodies and terrestrial bodies; but the glory of the celestial is one, and the glory of the terrestrial is another.*

41 *There is one glory of the sun, another glory of the moon, and another glory of the stars; for one star differs from another star in glory.*

42 *So also is the resurrection of the dead. The body is sown in corruption, it is raised in incorruption.*

43 *It is sown in dishonor, it is raised in glory. It is sown in weakness, it is raised in power.*

44 *It is sown a natural body, it is raised a spiritual body. There is a natural body, and there is a spiritual body.*

45 *And so it is written, "The first man Adam became a living being." The last Adam became a life-giving spirit.*

46 *However, the spiritual is not first, but the natural, and afterward the spiritual.*

47 *The first man was of the earth, made of dust; the second Man is the Lord from heaven.*

48 *As was the man of dust, so also are those who are made of dust; and as is the heavenly Man, so also are those who are heavenly.*

49 *And as we have borne the image of the man of dust, we shall also bear the image of the heavenly Man.*

50 *Now this I say, brethren, that flesh and blood cannot inherit the kingdom of God; nor does corruption inherit incorruption.*

51 *Behold, I tell you a mystery: We shall not all sleep, but we shall all be changed—*

52 *in a moment, in the twinkling of an eye, at the last trumpet. For the trumpet will sound, and the dead will be raised incorruptible, and we shall be changed.*

53 *For this corruptible must put on incorruption, and this mortal must put on immortality.*

54 *So when this corruptible has put on incorruption, and this mortal has put on immortality, then shall be brought to pass the saying that is written: "Death is swallowed up in victory."*

55 *"O Death, where is your sting? O Hades, where is your victory?"*

56 *The sting of death is sin, and the strength of sin is the law.*

57 *But thanks be to God, who gives us the victory through our Lord Jesus Christ.*

58 *Therefore, my beloved brethren, be steadfast, immovable, always abounding in the work of the Lord, knowing that your labor is not in vain in the Lord.*

EXPLORING THE MEANING

6) How does the hope of the resurrection and a glorified body motivate you to live for Christ today?

_____

_____

_____

_____

_____

7) Paul spoke of "forgetting" the things which are in the past (Phil. 3:13). Where is the healthy balance between obsessing over past events and failing to move on, and remembering and learning from our past?

_____

_____

_____

_____

_____

8) Paul urged the Philippians to follow his example (v. 17). What older, wiser believer can you imitate in the pursuit of Christlikeness?

_____

_____

_____

_____

_____

_____

9) How can the truth of our citizenship in heaven alter the way we live on earth?

_____

_____

_____

_____

_____

_____

Truth for Today

People who make an impact in the world invariably have a single-minded commitment to reaching their goals. Whether those goals are to conquer the world, succeed in business, or win a championship, they are willing to make whatever sacrifices are necessary to achieve them. On the other hand, those who are consumed with their own needs and comfort rarely accomplish much.

The same is true in the Christian life. There are no hidden secrets, gimmicks, or shortcuts to a life that makes an impact on the world for the truth of Jesus Christ. Such lives are the direct result of a maximum effort to reach the spiritual goals of Christlikeness in life and ministry. Many noble servants of God have suffered much to reach those goals. Many even paid with their lives. All had one thing in common—their own comfort was less important to them than being like the Lord Jesus Christ in this world. They left their mark on the church through their undying devotion to Him and their untiring efforts for His gospel.

REFLECTING ON THE TEXT

10) What are your personal goals for advancing in spiritual maturity? Do you have a workable plan for reaching those goals?

_____

_____

_____

_____

_____

11) Most great accomplishments are the result of doing little things faithfully over a long time. List three "small" things (a daily devotional time, memorizing two Bible verses a week, praying faithfully for lost family members and friends, and so on) you can begin doing daily that, over time, will make a big difference in your spiritual growth.

_____

_____

_____

_____

_____

12) Make the commitment to sit down with a Christian friend in the next twenty-four hours to talk through the issues raised in this lesson. Talk through plans to address some of your weaknesses. Commit to hold each other accountable.

_____

_____

_____

_____

_____

PERSONAL RESPONSE

Write out additional reflections, questions you may have, or a prayer.

11

SPIRITUAL STABILITY

DRAWING NEAR

When in your life have you been the strongest—spiritually speaking? What factors or practices do you feel gave your faith stability and strength at that time?

_____

_____

_____

_____

When in your spiritual journey have you felt the shakiest and most uncertain? Why?

_____

_____

_____

_____

THE CONTEXT

The issue of spiritual stability is very much on Paul's heart in Philippians 4:1–9. It is true that the Philippian church had a special bond with Paul. They alone supported him when he left Macedonia. Paul did not have to sharply rebuke them for wavering doctrinally (as he did the Galatians) or tolerating sin (as he did the Corinthians). But there are hints throughout the epistle of the destabilizing threats facing the Philippian congregation. They were experiencing persecution. There was a lack of unity. False teachers posed a threat. But perhaps the most serious threat facing the Philippians was the dispute between two prominent women in the congregation that threatened to split the church into rival factions. The situation was compounded by the failure of the elders and deacons to deal with it. As a result of those destabilizing factors, some of the Philippians had failed to trust God and had given way to anxiety.

Paul desired that his beloved Philippian congregation be unwavering and firm in the faith. From this passage emerge seven basic principles for developing and maintaining spiritual stability: cultivating harmony in the church fellowship, maintaining a spirit of joy, learning to be content, resting on a confident faith in the Lord, reacting to problems with thankful prayer, thinking on godly virtues, and obeying God's standard.

KEYS TO THE TEXT

Stand Fast: This is an imperative verb, a command with almost a military ring to it. Like soldiers in the front line, believers are commanded to hold their position while under attack (see Eph. 6:11, 13–14). They are not to collapse under persecution, then compromise; to fail under testing, then complain; or to yield to temptation, and then sin.

UNLEASHING THE TEXT

Read 4:1–9, noting the key words and definitions next to the passage.

beloved and longed-for (v. 1)—Paul reveals his deep affection for the Philippian believers. The Greek term for "longed-for" refers to the deep pain of separation from loved ones.

my joy and crown (v. 1)—Paul did not derive his joy from circumstances, but from his fellow believers in Philippi (see 1 Thess. 2:19, 20; 3:9). The Greek term for "crown" refers to the laurel wreath received by an athlete for winning a contest (1 Cor. 9:25) or by a person honored by his peers at a banquet as a symbol of success or a fruitful life. The Philippian believers were proof that Paul's efforts were successful (see 1 Cor. 9:2).

Philippians 4:1–9 (NKJV)

1 *Therefore, my beloved and longed-for brethren, my joy and crown, so stand fast in the Lord, beloved.*

2 *I implore Euodia and I implore Syntyche to be of the same mind in the Lord.*

3 *And I urge you also, true companion, help these women who labored with me in the gospel, with Clement also, and the rest of my fellow workers, whose names are in the Book of Life.*

I implore (v. 2)—The Greek term means "to urge," or "to appeal."

Euodia . . . Syntyche (v. 2)—These two women were prominent church members (v. 3), who may have been among the women meeting for prayer when Paul first preached the gospel in Philippi (Acts 16:13). Apparently, they were leading two opposing factions in the church, most likely over a personal conflict.

the same mind (v. 2)—Another possible translation is "harmony." Spiritual stability depends on the mutual love, harmony, and peace between believers. Apparently the disunity in the Philippian church was about to destroy the integrity of its testimony.

companion (v. 3)—The Greek word pictures two oxen in a yoke, pulling the same load. A companion is a partner or an equal in a specific endeavor—in this case a spiritual one. It is possible that this individual is unnamed, but it is best to take the Greek word translated "companion" as a proper name (*Syzygos*). He was likely one of the church elders (1:1).

with Clement (v. 3)—Nothing is known of him.

Book of Life (v. 3)—In eternity past, God registered all the names of His elect in that book which identifies those inheritors of eternal life (see Dan. 12:1; Mal. 3:16, 17; Luke 10:20; Rev. 17:8; 20:12).

4   *Rejoice in the Lord always. Again I will say, rejoice!*

5   *Let your gentleness be known to all men. The Lord is at hand.*

6   *Be anxious for nothing, but in everything by prayer and supplication, with thanksgiving, let your requests be made known to God;*

7   *and the peace of God, which surpasses all understanding, will guard your hearts and minds through Christ Jesus.*

8   *Finally, brethren, whatever things are true, whatever things are noble, whatever things are just, whatever things are pure, whatever things are lovely, whatever things are of good report, if there is any virtue and if there is anything praiseworthy—meditate on these things.*

gentleness (v. 5)—This refers to contentment with and generosity toward others. It can also refer to mercy or leniency toward the faults and failures of others. It can even refer to patience exhibited by someone who submits to injustice or mistreatment without retaliating. Graciousness with humility encompasses all the above.

at hand (v. 5)—This can refer to nearness in space or time. The context suggests nearness in space: the Lord encompasses all believers with His presence (Ps. 119:151).

Be anxious for nothing (v. 6)—Fret and worry indicate a lack of trust in God's wisdom, sovereignty, or power. Delighting in the Lord and meditating on His Word are a great antidote to anxiety (Ps. 1:2).

in everything (v. 6)—All difficulties are within God's purposes.

prayer and supplication, with thanksgiving . . . requests (v. 6)—Gratitude to God accompanies all true prayer.

peace of God (v. 7)—Inner calm or tranquillity is promised to the believer who has a thankful attitude based on unwavering confidence that God is able and willing to do what is best for His children (see Rom. 8:28).

surpasses all understanding (v. 7)—This refers to the divine origin of peace. It transcends human intellect, analysis, and insight (Isa. 26:3; John 16:33).

guard (v. 7)—A military term meaning "to keep watch over." God's peace guards believers from anxiety, doubt, fear, and distress.

hearts . . . minds (v. 7)—Paul was not making a distinction between the two—he was giving a comprehensive statement referring to the whole inner person. Because of the believer's union with Christ, He guards his inner being with His peace.

true (v. 8)—What is true is found in God (2 Tim. 2:25), in Christ (Eph. 4:20–21), in the Holy Spirit (John 16:13), and in God's Word (John 17:17).

noble (v. 8)—The Greek term means "worthy of respect." Believers are to meditate on whatever is worthy of awe and adoration, i.e., the sacred as opposed to the profane.

just (v. 8)—This refers to what is right. The believer is to think in harmony with God's divine standard of holiness.

pure (v. 8)—that which is morally clean and undefiled

lovely (v. 8)—The Greek term means "pleasing" or "amiable." By implication, believers are to focus on whatever is kind or gracious.

of good report (v. 8)—That which is highly regarded or thought well of; it refers to what is generally considered reputable in the world, such as kindness, courtesy, and respect for others.

in me (v. 9)—The Philippians were to follow the truth of God that Paul proclaimed, along with the example of that truth lived by Paul before them.

9 *The things which you learned and received and heard and saw in me, these do, and the God of peace will be with you.*

the God of peace (v. 9)—See 1 Corinthians 14:33. God is peace (Rom. 16:20; Eph. 2:14), makes peace with sinners through Christ (2 Cor. 5:18–20), and gives perfect peace in trouble (v. 7).

1) Describe Paul's relationship with the Philippians, using only verse 1.

2) What was going on in the church that concerned Paul (vv. 2–3)?

3) What is Paul's "recipe" for finding true peace?

4) Paul spells out the kind of thought life that will lead to a stable Christian experience (v. 8). What are the marks of that way of thinking?

thanksgiving for what you do have
Peace of mind & heart Knowing a loving God is
for you

5) How did Paul specifically challenge the Philippians in verse 9?

GOING DEEPER

For more insight on how to maintain a peaceful mindset in an anxious world, read the words of Christ in Matthew 6:25–34.

25 *"Therefore I say to you, do not worry about your life, what you will eat or what you will drink; nor about your body, what you will put on. Is not life more than food and the body more than clothing?*

26 *Look at the birds of the air, for they neither sow nor reap nor gather into barns; yet your heavenly Father feeds them. Are you not of more value than they?*

27 *Which of you by worrying can add one cubit to his stature?*

28 *"So why do you worry about clothing? Consider the lilies of the field, how they grow: they neither toil nor spin;*

29 *and yet I say to you that even Solomon in all his glory was not arrayed like one of these.*

30 *Now if God so clothes the grass of the field, which today is, and tomorrow is thrown into the oven, will He not much more clothe you, O you of little faith?*

31 *"Therefore do not worry, saying, 'What shall we eat?' or 'What shall we drink?' or 'What shall we wear?'*

32 *For after all these things the Gentiles seek. For your heavenly Father knows that you need all these things.*

33 *But seek first the kingdom of God and His righteousness, and all these things shall be added to you.*

34 *Therefore do not worry about tomorrow, for tomorrow will worry about its own things. Sufficient for the day is its own trouble."*

EXPLORING THE MEANING

6) What did Jesus command us to do and not do?

> *Do not worry*
> *Seek ye first the Kingdom of God*
> *& his righteousness*

7) With all the assurances of Scripture, why is peace such a rare commodity among so many believers?

8) Why is gentleness such an important factor in relationships in the church?

Truth for Today

A concern for believers' spiritual stability permeates the New Testament. After a Gentile church was founded at Antioch, the Jerusalem church sent Barnabas to them, who, "encouraged them all that with purpose of heart they should continue with the Lord" (Acts 11:23 NKJV). Thus, the first apostolic message to the fledgling Gentile church was to be spiritually stable. This is because spiritual instability leads to disappointment, doubt, discouragement, and ineffective witness. Unstable people are likely to be crushed by their trials. They are also susceptible to temptation. Anxious, fretful, worried, harried believers are also inherently unstable. Weak, struggling, unstable Christians need to build their strength on the foundation of what the Bible says about God. A failure to understand His nature and purposes results in a subsequent lack of confidence in Him. The shifting sands of shallow or faulty theology provide no stable footing for the believer.

Reflecting on the Text

9) How would following Philippians 4:8 lead to spiritual stability? What is required in training our minds to think this way?

_____

_____

_____

10) Paul says that God's peace "will guard your hearts and minds" from anxiety, doubt, and worry. This is a military term used of soldiers on guard duty. Just as soldiers protect a city, so God's peace guards and protects believers who confidently trust in Him. Is your mind guarded by God's peace, or is it infiltrated by fear, doubt, and false ideas? Write down the issues that are troubling you now.

_____

_____

_____

_____

11) What guidelines are given in Philippians 4 that relate to your prayer life and your thought life? What do you sense God nudging you to change?

_____

_____

_____

_____

_____

_____

PERSONAL RESPONSE

Write out additional reflections, questions you may have, or a prayer.

_____

_____

_____

_____

_____

_____

_____

_____

_____

_____

_____

_____

_____

_____

_____

12

THE SECRET OF CONTENTMENT

DRAWING NEAR

When in your life have you had the most—materially speaking? When have you had the least?

What do you remember about how you felt during those different times?

THE CONTEXT

Concluding this letter to his beloved Philippian congregation, Paul expressed his deeply felt gratitude to them. He had enjoyed a special relationship with them since the founding of the church at Philippi. At one point in Paul's ministry, they were the only church that had supported him financially. Now they had again sent him a gift, and this passage is Paul's thank-you note to them. Beneath the surface of Paul's expression of thanks to the Philippians is the picture of a man utterly content in spite of such severe circumstances. Paul knew how to rejoice in every circumstance and be free from anxiety and worry, because his heart was guarded by the peace of God and the God of peace. His example is especially relevant to our utterly discontented culture.

Five principles of contentment flow from this seemingly mundane conclusion to Paul's letter. A contented person is confident in God's providence, satisfied with little, independent from circumstances, strengthened by divine power, and preoccupied with the well-being of others.

KEYS TO THE TEXT

Content: The Greek term means "to be self-sufficient," "to be satisfied," or "to have enough." It indicates a certain independence and lack of need for help. Sometimes it was used to refer to a person who supported himself or herself without anyone's aid. Paul was saying, "I have learned to be sufficient in myself—yet not in myself as myself, but as indwelt by Christ." He elsewhere expressed that subtle distinction: "I have been crucified with Christ; it is no longer I who live, but Christ lives in me; and the life which I now live in the flesh I live by faith in the Son of God, who loved me and gave Himself for me" (Gal. 2:20 NKJV). Christ and contentment go together.

I Can Do All Things: This means "to be strong," "to have power," or "to have resources." The Greek text emphasizes the "all things" by placing it first in the sentence. Paul was strong enough to endure anything through Christ's strength. The apostle did not, of course, mean that he could physically survive indefinitely without food, water, sleep, or shelter. What he was saying is that when he reached the limit of his resources and strength, even to the point of death, he was infused with the strength of Christ. He could overcome the most dire physical difficulties because of the inner, spiritual strength God had given him.

UNLEASHING THE TEXT

Read 4:10–23, noting the key words and definitions next to the passage.

Philippians 4:10–23 (NKJV)

at last . . . you lacked opportunity (v. 10)—About ten years had passed since the Philippians first gave a gift to Paul to help meet his needs when he was first in Thessalonica (vv. 15–16). Paul was aware of their desire to continue to help, but he realized, within God's providence, that they had not had the "opportunity" (season) to help.

10 *But I rejoiced in the Lord greatly that now at last your care for me has flourished again; though you surely did care, but you lacked opportunity.*

11 *Not that I speak in regard to need, for I have learned in whatever state I am, to be content:*

whatever state I am (v. 11)—Paul defined the circumstances in the following verse.

12 *I know how to be abased, and I know how to abound. Everywhere and in all things I have learned both to be full and to be hungry, both to abound and to suffer need.*

13 *I can do all things through Christ who strengthens me.*

14 *Nevertheless you have done well that you shared in my distress.*

15 *Now you Philippians know also that in the beginning of the gospel, when I departed from Macedonia, no church shared with me concerning giving and receiving but you only.*

16 *For even in Thessalonica you sent aid once and again for my necessities.*

17 *Not that I seek the gift, but I seek the fruit that abounds to your account.*

18 *Indeed I have all and abound. I am full, having received from Epaphroditus the things sent from you, a sweet-smelling aroma, an acceptable sacrifice, well pleasing to God.*

19 *And my God shall supply all your need according to His riches in glory by Christ Jesus.*

abased . . . abound (v. 12)—Paul knew how to get along with humble means (food, clothing, daily necessities) and how to live in prosperity ("to overflow").

to be full and to be hungry (v. 12)—The Greek word translated "to be full" was used of feeding and fattening animals. Paul knew how to be content when he had plenty to eat and when he was deprived of enough to eat.

all things (v. 13)—Paul had strength to withstand both difficulty and prosperity in the material world.

through Christ who strengthens me (v. 13)—The Greek word for "strengthens" means "to put power in." Because believers are in Christ (Gal. 2:20), He infuses them with His strength to sustain them until they receive some provision (Eph. 3:16–20; 2 Cor. 12:10).

shared (v. 14)—to join in a partnership with someone

in the beginning of the gospel (v. 15)—when Paul first preached the gospel in Philippi (Acts 16:13)

when I departed (v. 15)—when Paul first left Philippi approximately ten years before (Acts 16:40)

Macedonia (v. 15)—In addition to Philippi, Paul also ministered in two other towns in Macedonia: Thessalonica and Berea (Acts 17:1–14).

concerning giving and receiving (v. 15)—Paul used three business terms. "Concerning" could be translated "account." "Giving and receiving" refer to expenditures and receipts. Paul was a faithful steward of God's resources and kept careful records of what he received and spent.

the fruit (v. 17)—The Greek word can be translated "profit."

abounds to your account (v. 17)—The Philippians were in effect storing up for themselves treasure in heaven (Matt. 6:20). The gifts they gave to Paul were accruing eternal dividends to their spiritual account (Prov. 11:24–25; 19:17; Luke 6:38; 2 Cor. 9:6).

a sweet-smelling aroma, an acceptable sacrifice, well-pleasing to God (v. 18)—In the Old Testament sacrificial system, every sacrifice was to provide a fragrant aroma and be acceptable to God. Only if it was offered with the correct attitude would it be pleasing to Him (Gen. 8:20–21; Ex. 29:18; Lev. 1:9, 13, 17). The Philippians' gift was a spiritual sacrifice (see Rom. 12:1; 1 Peter 2:5) that pleased God.

all your need (v. 19)—Paul addressed all of the Philippians' material needs, which had probably been depleted to some extent because of their gracious gift (Prov. 3:9).

according to His riches (v. 19)—God would give increase to the Philippians in proportion to His infinite resources, not just a small amount out of His riches.

every saint (v. 21)—Instead of using the collective "all," Paul used the individualistic "every" to declare that each saint was worthy of his concern.

brethren who are with me (v. 21)—They certainly included Timothy and Epaphroditus (2:19, 25). Others who were preaching the gospel in Rome were present (1:14). It is possible that Tychicus, Aristarchus, Onesimus, and Jesus Justus were also there (Col. 4:7, 9–11).

20 *Now to our God and Father be glory forever and ever. Amen.*

21 *Greet every saint in Christ Jesus. The brethren who are with me greet you.*

22 *All the saints greet you, but especially those who are of Caesar's household.*

23 *The grace of our Lord Jesus Christ be with you all. Amen.*

Caesar's household (v. 22)—A significant number of people, not limited to Caesar's family, which would include courtiers, princes, judges, cooks, food-tasters, musicians, custodians, builders, stablemen, soldiers, and accountants. Within that large group, Paul had in mind those who, through the proclamation of the gospel by members of the church at Rome, had been saved prior to his coming. Newly added to their number were those led to Christ by Paul himself, including those soldiers who were chained to him while he was a prisoner (1:13).

1) What are your overall impressions of this closing passage in Philippians? What truths jump out at you?

_____

_____

_____

_____

_____

2) What is revealed here about the Philippians' support of Paul's missionary work?

_____

_____

_____

_____

_____

_____

3) What insights do you gain into Paul's financial condition?

_____

_____

_____

_____

4) What prompted Paul's doxology of praise in verse 20?

_____

_____

_____

_____

_____

_____

GOING DEEPER

In a greedy, materialistic culture, it is easy for Christians to become discontented and obsessed with worldly wealth and possessions. Read 1 Timothy 6:6–19 for another reminder of what's true.

6 *Now godliness with contentment is great gain.*

7 *For we brought nothing into this world, and it is certain we can carry nothing out.*

8 *And having food and clothing, with these we shall be content.*

9 *But those who desire to be rich fall into temptation and a snare, and into many foolish and harmful lusts which drown men in destruction and perdition.*

10 *For the love of money is a root of all kinds of evil, for which some have strayed from the faith in their greediness, and pierced themselves through with many sorrows.*

11 *But you, O man of God, flee these things and pursue righteousness, godliness, faith, love, patience, gentleness.*

12 *Fight the good fight of faith, lay hold on eternal life, to which you were also called and have confessed the good confession in the presence of many witnesses.*

13 *I urge you in the sight of God who gives life to all things, and before Christ Jesus who witnessed the good confession before Pontius Pilate,*

14 *that you keep this commandment without spot, blameless until our Lord Jesus Christ's appearing,*

15 *which He will manifest in His own time, He who is the blessed and only Potentate, the King of kings and Lord of lords,*

16 *who alone has immortality, dwelling in unapproachable light, whom no man has seen or can see, to whom be honor and everlasting power. Amen.*

17 *Command those who are rich in this present age not to be haughty, nor to trust in uncertain riches but in the living God, who gives us richly all things to enjoy.*

18 *Let them do good, that they be rich in good works, ready to give, willing to share,*

19 *storing up for themselves a good foundation for the time to come, that they may lay hold on eternal life.*

Exploring the Meaning

5) What important principles does 1 Timothy 6 contain about the subject of money and contentment?

_____

_____

_____

_____

6) The contented attitude of someone like Paul is incomprehensible to today's society. Instead, people are obsessed with delineating their needs and wants, and loudly demanding that they be met. How, realistically and practically, can Christians avoid this trap?

_____

_____

_____

_____

_____

7) How have you experienced the truth of Philippians 4:13?

_____

_____

_____

_____

_____

_____

_____

8) The theme of the concluding paragraph of the book of Philippians is found in the word *saint* (vv. 21–22). What does the term really mean, and to whom does it apply?

_____

_____

_____

_____

_____

_____

Truth for Today

Contentment is a highly prized but elusive virtue. It comes only from being rightly related to God and trusting His sovereign, loving, purposeful providence. Nevertheless, people seek it where it cannot be found—in money, possessions, power, prestige, relationships, jobs, or freedom from difficulties. But by that definition contentment is unattainable, for it is impossible in this fallen world to be completely free from problems.

In sharp contrast to the world's understanding of contentment is this simple definition of spiritual contentment penned by the Puritan Jeremiah Burroughs: "Christian contentment is that sweet, inward, quiet, gracious frame of spirit, which freely submits to and delights in God's wise and fatherly disposal in every condition."

Reflecting on the Text

9) List some specific things you can do this week to cultivate an attitude of contentment.

_____

_____

_____

_____

10) Like the Philippians, how can you further the work of God by giving generously to His faithful servants? In addition to supporting the ongoing work of your church, what missionaries can you assist financially?

_____

_____

_____

_____

11) In how many different ways can you identify Paul's emphasis on joy throughout this letter?

_____

_____

_____

_____

_____

_____

_____

_____

Personal Response

Write out additional reflections, questions you may have, or a prayer.

Additional Notes

ADDITIONAL NOTES

ADDITIONAL NOTES

Additional Notes

Additional Notes

Additional Notes

ADDITIONAL NOTES

Additional Notes

Additional Notes

The MacArthur Bible Study Series

Revised and updated, the MacArthur Study Guide Series continues to be one of the bestselling study guide series on the market today. For small group or individual use, intriguing questions and new material take the participant deeper into God's Word.

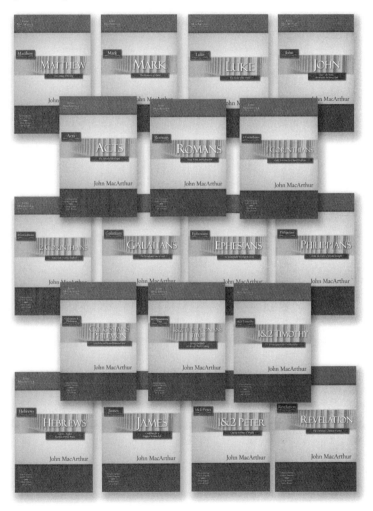

Available at your local Christian Bookstore or www.thomasnelson.com

Look for these exciting titles by John MacArthur

Experiencing the Passion of Christ

Experiencing the Passion of Christ Student Edition

Twelve Extraordinary Women Workbook

Twelve Ordinary Men Workbook

Welcome to the Family:
What to Expect Now That You're a Christian

What the Bible Says About Parenting:
Biblical Principles for Raising Godly Children

Hard to Believe Workbook:
The High Cost and Infinite Value of Following Jesus

The John MacArthur Study Library for PDA

The MacArthur Bible Commentary

The MacArthur Study Bible, NKJV

The MacArthur Topical Bible, NKJV

The MacArthur Bible Commentary

The MacArthur Bible Handbook

The MacArthur Bible Studies series

Available at your local Christian bookstore
or visit www.thomasnelson.com

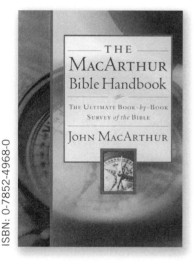
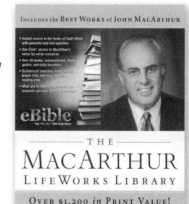